HAPPY CATHOLIC

Glimpses of God in Everyday Life Glimpses of God in Everyday Life Glimpses of God in Everyday Life Glimpses of God in Everyday Life Glimpses of God in Everyday Life Glimpses of God in Everyday Life Glimpses of God in Everyday Life. **JULIE DAVIS**

SERVANT
BOOKS

PUBLISHED BY ST. ANTHONY MESSENGER PRESS
CINCINNATI, OHIO

D0109479

Cover and book design by Mark Sullivan.

LIBRARY OF CONGRESS CATALOGING-IN-PUBLICATION DATA
Davis, Julie (Julianne Barbara), 1957–
Happy Catholic : glimpses of God in everyday life / Julie Davis.
p. cm.
Includes bibliographical references and index.
ISBN 978-0-86716-974-4 (alk. paper)
1. Christian life—Catholic authors. I. Title.
BX2350.3.D385 2011
248.4'82—dc22

2011002001

ISBN 978-0-86716-974-4

Published by Servant Books,
an imprint of St. Anthony Messenger Press
28 W. Liberty St.
Cincinnati, OH 45202
www.AmericanCatholic.org
www.ServantBooks.org

Printed in the United States of America.
Printed on acid-free paper.

11 12 13 14 15   5 4 3 2 1

With all my love for Tom,
who knew what I needed to come alive
and gave me the freedom to grasp it.

C O N T E N T S

Getting Here From There

> I was sitting in my car yesterday morning praying. Living that joy-
> ous sorrow I've been given. "I'm sorry for it, for the hatred and
> contempt, the cross, the whip, the nails...." And Jesus says to me
> with great joy, "I'm not! I'm not sorry at all! I did it for you; you're
> worth it. For I have made you so."
>
> I do not look around and the world is made new; the world
> is the same as it ever was. But I am a new creation and I look
> around with new eyes. This is what my God has given me; this
> is what his church has given me....
>
> > New convert and commenter,
> > *Catholic and Enjoying It* blog

Precisely.

The blinders have fallen from my eyes, and I can hardly believe
the depth and layers of meaning that are in evidence all around us.

Why did it take me so long to see the truth that floods through
everyday life? Every time I look back at where I began and where I
am now, I am astounded.

My parents were what I think of as the good, old-fashioned sort of
atheists. Religion was silly superstition, so why argue about it? We
were taught to be good people and that, as long as you didn't break
the law or hurt anyone, what you did was your own business.

This didn't mean that I didn't wonder if God existed. I just didn't know how anyone could ever be sure that God was real. I grew up, married, and had children. The whole time I kept wondering.

Then, God used what I cared about most to get my attention.

Halfway through our oldest daughter's kindergarten class, irreconcilable differences between Hannah and her teacher required leaving public school. (Don't ask. Just know that it wasn't the five-year-old's fault.) She began attending the local Catholic school. One day the religion teacher told the children that anyone who wasn't attending Sunday Mass needed to go home and tell their parents that they needed to attend. Hannah did not simply pass the message on. As only a kindergartner can, she dug in her heels and insisted on proper behavior. Pretty soon we were attending weekly Mass at St. Thomas.

Now I really couldn't avoid the question of God's existence. Most of the "proof" I ever heard seemed like simple coincidence to me. Weekly Mass gave me plenty of thinking time, and finally I came up with a plan to force God's hand.

We desperately needed a larger house, but no one would even make an offer on ours. Kneeling at Mass I made God a deal. All he had to do was to get me a new house as a sign. Then I'd know he was there. And I'd have a new house. Clever, eh?

Of course, nothing happened. Finally, after about a year had gone by, I realized that something inside me had changed. It wasn't because of any dramatic feeling or discovery, but I didn't need that proof I had wanted. Kneeling at Mass once again, I told God that I'd just take his existence on faith. I told him that he didn't need to pay off. I was fine as I was.

The next day our new accountant found major tax errors that garnered a refund big enough for a new house. We found a perfect house that had been on the market for months with the price just lowered to what we could afford. Two weeks later our house was sold without ever going on the market. The buyer was determined to have a house with the exact specifications of ours within a six-block area that we were smack-dab in the middle of. All the realtors said they had never seen anything like the smooth progress of the sale and our purchase.

I don't believe in coincidence anymore.

Five years later, I went through RCIA and became Catholic during the Easter Vigil of 2000. I love it. I love the traditions, I love the saints, I love the Eucharist.... I love being Catholic.

One of the things that made my conversion so powerful to me, in retrospect, is that it was so personal. This was all just between God and me. I didn't discuss it with my husband, and I didn't even read any books about religion. In fact, although I'd always been an avid reader, it never even occurred to me that they "had" books about religion.

After my confirmation, though, I was given a Catholic book, and that began a reading frenzy. I began seeing a pattern of truth and beauty that I never knew existed. Soon, everywhere I looked, I recognized the pattern. Books I read, movies I watched, songs I heard were reflecting bits of the Truth that was God. I realized that this reality had been there all along. I just couldn't see it before. It made everyday things glow. I couldn't hold in my delight and began e-mailing friends with my discoveries. The e-mails turned into a blog, Happy Catholic, which reflected everything I loved about being Catholic every day.

This book continues that sharing.

We see echoes of heaven all around us, sometimes without ever knowing what we are seeing. I have a passion for quotes that point toward those truths. That passion turned into short reflections on some of my favorite quotes. You'll find everything here from movies to television to Scripture, from humor to seriousness to optimism and joy. In short, everything that draws back the veil and lets us connect with God. I hope it delights you as much as it does me.

Julie Davis
The Feast of St. Martha (my patient patron)

Flinching Before God

> We are not necessarily doubting that God will do the best for
> us; we are wondering how painful the best will turn out to be.
>
> C.S. Lewis

Mother Teresa serving the poor in Calcutta. Pope John Paul II,
twisted with pain, unable to speak in his illness and old age. God
saying, "This is how I treat my friends, Teresa," after St. Teresa of
Avila was dumped into a large mud puddle. We are in full sympathy
when she answers, "No wonder you have so few of them, Lord!" It
isn't just the world that is wary of what it means to really serve God.
We, too, tend to lean back a little when we feel that God might be
calling us forward for a special task.

Lately, however, I have begun to feel that we have it all wrong.
Those times that I have truly been closest to God, I have had no
problem tackling things that normally would cause me grave appre-
hension. It is not a matter of what God "inflicts" so much as how
aligned we are with him, how much we are willing to give.

God knows us better than we know ourselves. He created us to be
who we are and achieve perfectly the place we inhabit in life. So why
would we not thrill to our task, find it fascinating and enthralling, be
pulled back to it time and again? Yes, it may take us beyond what we
plan or think we can do, push us out of the comfortable places where

we live. Merely being willing to step into that potential discomfort is part of the growth we need to see God's plan falling into place bit by slow bit.

Such are God's ways and such is our own reluctant recognition of our own shortsightedness that we read C.S. Lewis and wryly laugh in acknowledgment. And then, hopefully, press on past the doubt.

. | . | . | . | . | .

Jesus in the Rearview Mirror

> **God:** Bender, being God isn't easy. If you do too much, people get dependent on you. And if you do nothing, they lose hope. You have to use a light touch, like a safecracker or a pickpocket.
>
> **Bender:** Or a guy who burns down a bar for the insurance money.
>
> **God:** Yes, if he makes it look like an electrical thing. If you do things right, people won't be sure you've done anything at all.
>
> *Futurama*

We are so often left like Moses, who asked to see God but only saw his hindquarters (see Exodus 33:23). We see evidence of God only in hindsight. Even then it can be very difficult to tell definitively that there was divine intervention unless you are the person for whom the miracle was done. Anyone who has experienced a miracle will tell you that when God sends you a message you recognize it, even though others might not. Others are measuring by verifiable results. You are experiencing something that cannot be measured. Miracles are love letters.

The Lover and the beloved understand. It is enough.

. | . | . | . | . | .

Everything Old Is New Again

> Late have I loved Thee, O Beauty, so ancient and so new; late
> have I loved Thee! For behold Thou were within me and I out-
> side and in my unloveliness fell upon those lovely things Thou
> has made. Thou were with me and I was not with Thee. I was
> kept from Thee by those things, yet had they not been in Thee,
> they would not have been at all. Thou did call and cry to me
> and break open my deafness; and Thou did send forth Thy
> beams and shine upon me and chase away my blindness; Thou
> did breathe fragrance upon me, and I drew in my breath and
> do now pant for Thee; I tasted Thee and now hunger and thirst
> for Thee; Thou did touch me, and I have burned for Thy peace.
>
> St. Augustine

This stopped me in my tracks when I first read it soon after enter-
ing the Church. How had this man gotten it so right? "I drew in my
breath and do now pant for Thee."

You would have to look very hard to find an ancient who would fit
better into our pleasure-loving world than Augustine before his
conversion. Back in 400 AD Augustine was a bright, intense ne'er-
do-well who broke his devout Christian mother's heart as he drifted
from heresy to heresy in search of God. The man whose prayer was
"God make me chaste, but not yet" had a longtime mistress and
teenage love child when he suddenly had an encounter with God.
That encounter set him on the path that gave us a defender of the
faith, a loving bishop to the people of Hippo, and one of the greatest
doctors of the Church.

He said it well for every convert. Like all of us, he had no idea that God had been using even St. Augustine's wayward times to prepare him to do God's work.

Reread St. Augustine's words. Think of your encounters with God. Then, step forward in faith for a deeper encounter with that Beauty, so ancient and so new.

· | · | · | · | · | ·

Gonna Wash That Gray Right Outta My Soul

"There's no grays, only white that's got grubby. I'm surprised you don't know that. And sin, young man, is when you treat people as things. Including yourself. That's what sin is" [said Granny Weatherwax].

"It's a lot more complicated than that" [said Brother Oat].

"No. It ain't. When people say things are a lot more complicated than that, they means they're getting worried that they won't like the truth. People as things, that's where it starts."

"Oh, I'm sure there are worse crimes…"

"But they starts with thinking about people as things."

Terry Pratchett, *Carpe Jugulum*

Did you know that the Ten Commandments are actually all about relationships? The first three are about our relationship with God, and the last seven are about our relationships with other people.

Those basic rules that seem so nitpicky are really there as a positive force to help us love God and each other. God doesn't need them. He is pure love. On the other hand, we surely do need them. It's not as if they're difficult to understand. No wonder Jesus could sum them up so simply in two sentences: "You shall love the Lord, your God, with all your heart, with all your soul, and with all your mind.... You shall love your neighbor as yourself. The whole law and the prophets depend on these two commandments" (Matthew 22:37, 39–40).

It is interesting that Terry Pratchett, an atheist, writes hugely popular books that also happen to do a splendid job of telling us the truths that count while shining light on our foibles. That's enough to make you realize that sin and virtue are part of human nature. It's certainly enough to help us recognize them as universal truths transcending the grubby lines between faith and unbelief.

. | . | . | . | . | .

It Don't Come Easy

> The parents of these young soldiers would come to me and ask me how the Lord could allow such a thing. I felt like asking them what the Lord would have to do to tell us He didn't *allow* something.
>
> Marilynne Robinson, *Gilead*

It don't come easy because we don't let it.

Why is it that we are so willing to attribute the bad things in life to God's plan? Any lesser creature than God would surely weep when looking upon the grim things that we do to each other with free will and full consent. It doesn't have to be anything as drastic as war or crime, either. Sometimes a selfish reaction or harsh word is enough to set off a chain reaction in another's soul that has unintended consequences. However, our culpability is no less for all our lack of intention.

We're not the first to ask why God has allowed something bad to happen. We see it time and again in the Bible: "Why has the Lord permitted us to be defeated today?" (1 Samuel 4:3). The entire book of Job is dedicated to examining the question of why bad things happen to good people. Indeed, throughout history, no matter what their faith, people must have asked that selfsame question.

God can surely bring good out of evil. He does it all the time. Yet how much better, how much easier would it be on us if he didn't have to go through all the machinations necessary to fix things when we put them wrong? What is it that I can cooperate with right now that will smooth the way? It is for these questions that self-examination was invented.

· | · | · | · | · | ·

As We Forgive Those Who Trespass Against Us...

> Murphy, who was more or less Catholic, frowned. "Seems to me that Christianity has a few things to say about forgiveness and tolerance and treating others the way you'd like to be treated."
>
> "Uh huh," I said. "Then comes the Crusades, the Inquisition..."
>
> "Which is my point," Murphy said. "Regardless of what I think of Islam or Wicca or any other religion, the fact is that it's a group of people. Every faith has its ceremonies. And since it's made up of people, every faith also has its [jerks]."
>
> Jim Butcher, *White Night*

Those are the ones that drive you crazy. The jerks. The ones who can't let go of the small stuff. The ones who are loud and obnoxious. The ones who don't think about anyone except themselves, even when they fool themselves (and often others) that they are putting God first. Because people are people. There's no getting around that fact. They're out there, everywhere, and making it tough for the rest of us. Worse yet, they are often Christians who are the subjects of the evening news, giving the rest cause to cringe as we acquire guilt by association.

This is a good occasion for prayer. Yes, we must pray even for that darned jerk. It's hard sometimes, but our own attitudes toward those people who offend us most ("...as we forgive those who trespass against us...") is what we find ourselves needing to deal with most. In fact, knowing human nature, we can just go ahead and count on the fact that we're going to need forgiveness ourselves sooner rather than later. Jesus knew that fact so well that he even gave us the words to use in the prayer he taught us himself: "Forgive us our trespasses as we forgive those who trespass against us."

I always try to remember that for every person driving me crazy, there may be two others that I am driving crazy. Ouch!

· | · | · | · | · | ·

A Really Good Prayer

Lord, have mercy on me and bless them.

This is a prayer that never fails. It is excellent for those times when someone is crunching popcorn in your ear while you are watching *The Passion*, when the choir won't stop practicing even though they did not reserve the room that you need to use, or when you find yourself in the situation I did the other day, talking to a very angry man who treated me contemptuously as a simple fool. In other words, it is perfect for dealing with the irritations of daily life.

This simple prayer is proof that you do not have to "feel" the prayer. You simply must be willing to say it, however grudgingly. Considering the circumstances that lead up to it, I always am upset and irritated whenever I say it. Do I actually want those annoying people to be blessed? Humph, I should say not! (At least I don't feel as if I do, although I am going to the effort of saying the prayer.)

In fact, the other day I was shaking with anger when I suddenly realized that prayer was running over and over in my head. However, it is the classic case of "ask and you shall receive." Whenever I say it, I never fail to be reminded of my many imperfections, my pride, and that we are all sinners together. Often that is just what I need to calm down and let my anger go. When that happens it is all grace, an amazing triumph over my worst instincts, an answer to prayer for which I am very grateful.

Thanks be to God for that simple prayer and his quick answers.

· | · | · | · | · | ·

Person-to-Person

> Then I heard the voice of the Lord saying, "Whom shall I send? Who will go for us?" "Here I am," I said; "send me!"
>
> Isaiah 6:8

> You duped me, O LORD, and I let myself be duped.... I say to myself, I will not mention him, I will speak in his name no more. But then it becomes like fire burning in my heart, imprisoned in my bones; I grow weary holding it in, I cannot endure it.
>
> Jeremiah 20:7, 9

I'm not unique in feeling that both Isaiah and Jeremiah speak for me when I read those words. There is a reason they are among the most quoted and beloved of scriptural quotations among striving Christians. I first encountered them after a retreat that was instrumental in breaking through barriers of selfishness and blame, in healing hurt and granting me graces to carry me forward. These words defined that experience in a way that touches me to this day.

What I like about the personal aspect is that it shows how intimately God knows us, how directly he cares about our guidance and support. What I like about the universal Christian experience of those Scriptures is that, for all our individuality, we are all alike in our longing and need for God's touch. We all have those impulsive moments of throwing ourselves forward: "Here I am. Send me." This is often followed by the dismay of seeing the mountains that must be scaled to accomplish our tasks, "You duped me, O LORD, and I let myself be duped." (Some scholars say a better translation than "duped" is "seduced." Now, that is a fact worth thinking about for a while.)

Like Jesus, we may pray that the cup be taken from us, but it is in doing God's will in the big tasks that we discover what the grace of God is really all about. That our weakness is supplied by his strength. That we control nothing, but that with God all things are possible. Nothing is like that experience, and we must live it to grasp it, even slightly. We learn to know ourselves better; we fall in love more deeply with God.

· | · | · | · | · | ·

Still Countercultural After All These Years

Drinking beer is easy. Trashing your hotel room is easy. But being a Christian, that's a tough call. That's rebellion.

Alice Cooper

If you care about what people think of you, then you should not have become a Catholic.

St. John Vianney

It is astounding that as far as we have advanced, there is still nothing more shocking to the world than a faithful Christian. Jesus was radical in his time. Following Christ makes us radicals in turn. We're called on to slice through all those neat little boxes that people use to make things more understandable. There is no political party we can trust. There is no nation that gets it right. There is no cultural group where we are going to completely feel at home. We are the ultimate outsiders. That's OK, really. If we're doing it right, then we're upsetting things because we won't "settle" and we won't conform. We answer to a higher power.

Take another look at that crucifix and remember the only really original rebel, the one whose watchword of "Love one another" casts the world into confusion. Then prepare to be fully yourselves in Christ and watch the confusion spread, along with the love.

· | · | · | · | · | ·

Wherever You Go, There You Are*

Reality check: you can never, ever, use weight loss to solve problems that are not related to your weight. At your good weight or
not, you still have to live with yourself and deal with your problems. You still have the same husband, the same job, the same
kids, and the same life. Losing weight is not a cure for life.

Phillip McGraw (Dr. Phil)

If it isn't weight loss, then it's a face-lift. Or perhaps a new house. A
higher salary. Personally, I never met a cookbook that wasn't going
to make me a more varied, better cook who lovingly prepared
evening meals every single night, no matter how harried my day has
been. And that will make me a better mother.

Won't it?

Let's face facts. The change we need is internal, in our hearts and
souls. Or should we say that the change we need is eternal? So much
of the time those big changes we crave are just external expressions
of our longing and need for something we can only get by the grace
of God. I can't leave myself behind. I need a makeover in many ways,
it is true, but they all begin with a good foundation. I'll never get that
without beginning by turning to Jesus and asking for him to trans-
form me from the inside out.

---

*I was surprised to find that this modern-sounding phrase came from a
venerable source and was attached to a distinctly Christian meaning:

So, the cross is always ready and waits for you everywhere. You cannot
escape it no matter where you run, for wherever you go you are burdened with yourself, and wherever you go, there you are.

Thomas à Kempis

· | · | · | · | · | ·

Across the Universe

"As you dig deeper and deeper into physics," I said to Collins, "do you have a sense of wonder and awe at what you find?"

"I really do," he said, a grin breaking on his face. "Not just with the fine-tuning but in lots of areas, like quantum mechanics and the ability of our minds to understand the world. The deeper we dig, we see that God is more subtle and more ingenious and more creative than we ever thought possible. And I think that's the way God created the universe for us—to be full of surprises."

Lee Strobel

I read this and was delighted and transformed. I love the idea of God planning surprises for us. What was the last thing that I discovered with such surprise? I'm not on those scientists' level. My discoveries are much more ordinary, yet simultaneously unique each time. My science is in the kitchen. My mathematics is applied in graphic design. My astronomy is nonexistent, although I feel a thrill of accomplishment every time I successfully locate Orion in the winter sky. Yet an elegant solution in any of these places gives its own unique pleasure.

Thinking back over my short time as a Christian, I know it to be true that God loves to surprise us. The next time I make a surprising discovery I am going to try to remember it as a reflection of God's fun-loving, gift-giving nature.

· | · | · | · | · | ·

It's Turtles All the Way Down*

Philosophy begins in wonder. And, at the end, when philosophic thought has done its best, the wonder remains.

Alfred North Whitehead

Probably one of the nicest things that my husband, Tom, has ever done was to give me this quote when he came across it, saying that it made him think of me.

This was after I had discovered that people actually wrote books about Catholicism (who knew!) and threw myself into them. I would come to the dinner table all lit up about something that St. Augustine had said or a new scriptural concept that had just been explained. Despite the technical mumbo jumbo in which I delighted, it was impossible to shake that sense of wonder and personal connection that had drawn me to my faith in the first place.

This proves, I think, that not only does Tom understand me; he appreciates one of the qualities that define me. What woman doesn't thrill to that?

---

* This works with the above on a couple of levels. Yes, it really does. Just let it sink in:

Dimitri: If Atlas holds up the world, what holds up Atlas?
Tasso: Atlas stands on the back of a turtle.
Dimitri: But what does the turtle stand on?
Tasso: Another turtle.
Dimitri: And what does that turtle stand on?
Tasso: My dear Dimitri, it's turtles all the way down!

Thomas Cathcart and Daniel Klein

· | · | · | · | · | ·

Hit Me With Your Best Shot

You understood the Jesus who turned water into wine at the wedding feast to save the young couple from embarrassment. You believed in that Jesus, the one who was kind and anonymously generous. But you never quite believed in the Jesus of the second half of that chapter [John 2] who braided a whip to drive the businessmen from the temple, who flung aside the tables of the money changers and scattered their cash and stampeded all their livestock.

Was there human blood on the whip when he was done, do you think? Or did he just wave the whip over his head like a baton twirler in a halftime show and request that all the nasty, bad men please leave the premises immediately?

Jesus wasn't Gandhi. Jesus said that when someone jolted your jaw, the right thing to do was look them calmly in the eye and stick out your chin to give them a clean swing at the other side. This is how a tiger says, "Is that your best shot? You want another swing? Here, let me make this easy for you."

Turning the other cheek isn't submissive. It's defiant....

Roy H. Williams

I never thought of "turning the other cheek" in these terms. But it fits somehow. As a way of standing up for something, of not lying down and taking it. It is the way that Jesus chose when he chose to give himself up for our salvation.

How many of you would have expected to hear this fiery talk of Christ from a businessman who usually podcasts about advertising? I know. Me neither. You don't have to always keep your eyes open for Christ in the real world. Sometimes he comes out swinging a two-by-four so we pay attention. Thanks, Roy H. Williams.

· | · | · | · | · | ·

Will You Respect Me After the March?

The first temptation, my dear brethren, which the devil tries on anyone who has begun to serve God better, is in the matter of human respect.

St. John Vianney

I have a degree of self-confidence now that I could only have dreamed of when I was a shy and retiring youngster. I worry much less about acceptance.

At least I thought I did until the day I was on my way back from the March for Life holding a sign I'd picked up to keep people from tripping over it. One side said, "Women Do Regret Abortion." The other side read, "Men Regret Lost Fatherhood."

Carrying that sign was all well and good when I was in the middle of over five thousand people who all felt the same way. However, getting on the homebound train with it was a different matter. Suddenly I was supremely self-conscious and worried that I was going to encounter someone who would make it a point to object.

I also knew just how complacent I'd been. How vain to think that I didn't care about other people's opinions. What an idiot.

Good thing that we sat right in the middle of a group of women who had been attending a Women of Faith conference. I felt so relieved when one woman asked what the sign said, I told her, and she gave me a thumbs-up.

I'm smart enough to know that wasn't just dumb luck. It was a not-so-subtle message against complacency. It was a reminder of how easy it is to ignore the fact that I am the one who is succumbing to temptation. I just wish these lessons would stick better so God didn't have to keep whapping me with them.

· | · | · | · | · | ·

As Honest as the Cat When the Meat's Out of Reach*

> God gave us cats so that we would have an example of how
> we treat Him—mainly that we totally ignore Him as we go
> about our lives, but when we want something we will start to
> purr and figuratively rub ourselves against His legs to gain his
> attention for our wants.
>
> Jeff Miller

Maybe I love this quote so much because I have long maintained that
the very things we laugh at in cats are the qualities that we have ourselves.

- Cats don't like getting wet unless it's their idea. Neither do we.
- Cats are pretty finicky. So are we, especially here in the good old
  U.S. of A.
- Cats don't like being surprised. Neither do we. (I have yet to find
  anyone who loves being on the receiving end of an April Fool's
  Day joke.)
- Cats are not shy about letting you know when you've made them
  mad. The modern lack of etiquette has made that a match for us
  also.
- Cats love warmth, being petted, and luxury. Do I have to say it?
  Of course we do.

We may not spend much time musing about our resemblance to
cats, but it's no wonder that Jeff Miller's comment about cats and
God hits home. You don't have to have seen the resemblance for it to
sting a little.

So we're like cats. As long as we know it, then we can deal with it.

We're also a lot like the French. But let's save that for another day....

*Old English saying. Surely you can guess the similarities here.

· | · | · | · | · | ·

My Way or the Highway

> Welcome anyone who is weak in faith, but not for disputes over opinions.
>
> One person believes that one may eat anything, while the weak person eats only vegetables.
>
> The one who eats must not despise the one who abstains, and the one who abstains must not pass judgment on the one who eats; for God has welcomed him.
>
> Romans 14:1–3
>
> Sadly, there are some little ones and weaker brothers who fancy themselves to be the strong ones, readily denouncing rather than just cautioning those interested in meat. Imagine a child lecturing an adult about matters requiring maturity and you might understand why some moviegoers roll their eyes when self-righteous Christians confront them on what they choose to watch. Their selections may be complicated and even dangerous, but that does not always mean that the viewers are spiritually ignorant or rebellious.
>
> Jeffrey Overstreet

Clearly I like meat.

I have found an amazing freedom in the Catholic Church, not only an overwhelming freedom from my past sins and guilt but also the freedom to anticipate an intriguing future in which I would have a Helper through every kind of trouble.

Whenever I encounter Catholics who want to restrict a perfectly innocent pastime like movie watching or trick-or-treating, it makes me stand up for that "worldly pop culture." I constantly have to remind myself to practice charity, because I tend to stand up pretty strongly. Not only are the abstainers not to judge the strong, but the strong are not to despise the abstainers.

Hard words to live by. In Paul's day and in ours. Human nature just doesn't change much, does it?

· | · | · | · | · | ·

The Dog Ate My Homework

> An excuse is worse and more terrible than a lie: For an excuse
> is a lie guarded.
>
> Alexander Pope

To feel the full truth of this statement, do this: Go to confession and simply state your sins. No reasons. No excuses. Just state your sins. I can tell you this is brutally difficult and requires a will of iron. Of course, that might say more about me than anything else.

Non-Catholics may emulate this by envisioning making apologies similarly.

There is, of course, a difference between an honest reason or misunderstanding and an excuse. We know the difference. So does God. If we make excuses, are we fooling him?

No.

Only ourselves.

· | · | · | · | · | ·

I Can See Clearly Now

> A man asked a priest, "Is it OK if I smoke while I pray?" The
> priest said no—that would be disrespectful. A bit later he asked,
> "Can I pray while I smoke?" The priest said yes, pray all the
> time.
>
> An oft-told anecdote

Intentions and perspective. They make all the difference in the
world. Do I see them clearly?

· | · | · | · | · | ·

Natural-Born Skimmer

> Commander Adama: I don't lend books.
>
> Battlestar Galactica

For me it's always been all about books. A favorite book welcomes
you like an old friend, ready to share remembered pleasures with
some unnoticed facet often coming to light to deepen your appreciation. Of course, that is partly due to the fact that I'm a natural-born
skimmer, which means I read insanely fast, especially during cru-
cial passages. This lends itself to repeated readings, since I then can
slow down to savor missed details.

All this is to say that, like Captain Adama, I don't lend books. I
have sad little stories about favorite books that were borrowed and
then not simply lost but, as one woman blithely told me, sold at a
garage sale.

Sold. My book. At her garage sale.

Exercising exceptional restraint, I did not show her to the door. I did not comment upon this horrifying act. We are still friends. I do keep a careful eye on her if she lingers near one of my bookcases though.

There is one type of book, however, that I give away with a glad heart. These are my theology books. This is not because I don't love them. I certainly do. However, if there is even the slightest chance that someone will suddenly recognize a bit of the divine, feel that they are even a bit closer to God, or see their path a little more clearly, then who am I to get in the way? In fact, there are a few books I have "loaned" so many times that I keep a few on hand just so I can give them away whenever the need arises.

So, no, I don't lend books. I do give them away though, gladly.

· | · | · | · | · | ·

That's Amore

> We all know how much the King [Elvis Presley] wanted to be like Dean Martin.
>
> Bob Dylan

What?

Elvis wanted to be like Dino?

I was incredulous when I heard this, but I later heard Dean Martin's daughter, Deana, talking about how Elvis would ride his motorcycle up and down the street in front of their house. In fact, the King of Rock and Roll dubbed Dean Martin the King of Cool.

It's funny that no matter how high we rise, there always seems to be someone else who has what we really think we want. Is it that we have a built-in detector telling us there's always someone who really has it together, isn't hiding a fatal flaw, isn't as self-conscious as we are, doesn't lie to himself about anything? Of course we do. We have simply set our sights too low.

We're not looking for the King of Rock and Roll or even the King of Cool.

We're just looking for the King. You know which one I mean.

The One who makes a monarchist out of us all.

· | · | · | · | · | ·

Love and Potato Salad

> Somehow in rural Southern culture, food is always the first thought of neighbors when there is trouble.... "Here, I brought you some fresh eggs for breakfast. And here's a cake and some potato salad." It means "I love you. And I am sorry for what you are going through and I will share as much of the burden as I can." And maybe potato salad is a better way of saying it.
>
> Will D. Campbell

> The truth is that most bereaved souls crave nourishment more tangible than prayers: They want a steak. What is more, they need a steak.
>
> M.F.K. Fisher

We all like to think that grief or any other noble emotion for that matter elevates us past the petty requirements of the body. It does not take long for our bodies to cry out and remind us that we are separating them from our souls in a most unnatural manner.

Mysterious as it is, there is an undeniable connection. There is something recuperative in the right food at the right time. Some of it, naturally enough, is that we must have dinner no matter how sad we are. Bodily resources must be replenished. At the same time it lifts our spirits. Who among us has not experienced the laughter, stories, and tears that a funeral dinner brings? We cannot have that light lifting without the baked funeral meats as well. (If you're in Texas, barbecue does just as well.)

However, when our sustenance was brought by a friend or loved one who cared enough to take the trouble to provide that dinner, we are touched on a deeper level. It is a tangible reminder that they love us enough to spend precious time to reach out, make sure we know they are there with us in spirit, and take care of us as best they can.

Surely it is the noblest use of potato salad ever conceived by man.

· | · | · | · | · | ·

Turn the Movie Off

> This is the secret of peace, after committing a fault. What is past is past. And if we accept the consequences, while bracing our will, we can be sure that God will know how to draw glory even from our faults. Not to be downcast after committing a fault is one of the marks of true sanctity, for the saint knows how to find God in everything, in spite of human appearances. Once your will is sincerely "good," then don't worry.
> ...Our part is to bring ourselves into line with grace.
>
> Dom Augustin Guillerand, O. Cart.

I know I'm not the only person who reruns that little movie of the mind, replaying endlessly my thoughtless words, selfish moments, callous behavior, and more. It is like torture to review those moments, and yet I leave the movie running.

Is it that I like to hurt myself? Is it that I am not sorry? More usually it is that I am haunted by my imperfections. I can't ignore the fact either that I usually care most when there were witnesses to see me at my worst. Shouldn't I care even when there was no one except myself there? After all, as a friend once told me, God and the angels see every act.

The more I make myself aware that I'm rerunning the movie, the greater my ability to remember to turn to God. I turn to him not so much for forgiveness, although I surely need that on many occasions, but for the power to accept humbly the reality about my imperfect self. I turn to him for the grace to give myself the forgiveness which he gives freely.

It is then and only then that I can lean forward and click that movie off. It is then that I truly know who I am and fully accept God's forgiveness. It is then that I know that he loves me anyway, while telling me to go and sin no more.

. | . | . | . | . | .

I'm Not That Big a Yokel

"Pocket," she said after a moment.

"Yes, ma'am?"

"Pocket, you like women, don't you?"

He smiled a little. "Why yes, ma'am, I like women."

"Some men wouldn't, after what happened to you."

He shook his head. "Country stuff. I'm not that big a yokel."

"What do you mean, country stuff?"

"Oh, Miss Kendra, I've seen them. One crop fails and they say nothing will grow around here. Some Frenchman comes

along selling tools, then he rides off with the money and the tools
fall apart and folks say, 'See now, this proves all Frenchmen are
a bunch of swindlers.'" Pocket spoke contemptuously. "They see
one and they think they've seen it all. Country stuff." He looked
at her directly, across his whiskers. "Don't you be like that, Miss
Kendra."

Gwen Bristow, Calico Palace

Obviously we must learn from our experiences. How often do we let
one example become the rule rather than looking at the big picture
to see if it is, rather, the exception? How often do we skate the shallow surface rather than looking into the depths?

It's funny how often this crops up. The odd thing is that this never
comes up on the positive side of things. "That Frenchman helped
me out. How nice all Frenchmen are." I myself have experienced a
number of kind French people when traveling in France. Yet it
doesn't occur to me to take that as the norm rather than the exception.

What does it say about us if we only want to see the negative and
take such a small sample to prove it?

Yokels.

· | · | · | · | · | ·

The Ultimate Recycling

We all suffer. Some suffer well, some poorly, some bitterly, some
in union with Christ, some in union with our Lady and the Saints,
some in union with God as they know Him, some only in union
with the other people in the hospital and some all alone—but

we suffer. How much better it is to suffer even poorly and incon-
sistently in union with Christ.

Fr. Benedict Groeschel

I watched my parents as their health worsened. They thought God a
myth. They were angry and sad and hopeless and suffering. To see
their suffering going to waste broke my heart.

It is good to remember that each instance of suffering, large and
small, can be offered to Christ to use in helping break the cycle of
suffering for us all. Not only does Christ use it for others, but somehow it also makes my suffering less. Is it all in my head? I don't
think so. Somehow, at the human level, it removes the resentment
that suffering generates. I feel my suffering isn't wasted. It serves a
purpose.

It is a strange economy, this Catholic coin of using our suffering
to pay the way for others.

In the end my parents' story brightened. They realized that God
was something more than mythology.

They met him themselves in the midst of their suffering. It made
all the difference.

We all suffer. How much better indeed to suffer in union with
Christ.

· | · | · | · | · | ·

That Special Thrill

I have called you by name—you are mine.

Isaiah 43:1

Does this give you the same little thrill it gives me? Put a smile on
your face? Make you hold your head just a little bit higher?

Images flow all over television, selling us this way or that to make ourselves unique, special, one-of-a-kind. Brighter teeth, a luxury car, or what about a nice tattoo? It's the American way—showing our individuality in a way that is still somehow just like everyone else.

Yet right in front of us is the open love letter from God. We are cherished. "I have called you by name...."

It's not about stuff. It's about relationship. God and me. God and you. One on one. "You are mine."

. | . | . | . | . | .

Slow Down, You Move Too Fast

Miracle Max: You rush a miracle man, you get lousy miracles.

The Princess Bride

I am naturally impatient. Like most Americans, like most people that I know, actually, I decide upon a course of action and want it carried out immediately. Problem solved. Results achieved. Move on to the next thing.

How extremely annoying, then, that God has made me wait so many times for what I really want. He doesn't care if I am annoyed, because he turns out spectacular results. It takes time to get everything aligned for finding a spouse, having a baby—oh, and let's not forget a little thing like having God affirm his existence to me.

I have to face it. The problem is not with God. It is with me. How many times do I have to see it demonstrated? How long before I slow down, calm down, and trust?

I'm getting there.

Slowly.

· | · | · | · | · | ·

The Only Interesting Thing

> [The prioress] said, next, as to you and this story you have told
> me: you have been cruelly treated and betrayed, your child-
> hood has been stolen. The world is oftentimes une pâtisse'
> émerdée , a s*** pie, but this is known, this is boring. The only
> interesting thing is how we use the suffering that is inevitable in
> life.
>
> Michael Gruber, *Valley of Bones*

It is not very popular these days to think that suffering is
inevitable in life. Yet who among us has not known heartbreak,
loss, betrayal, or despair? It is part of the human condition. We
know it shouldn't be because we keep looking for ways around it,
saying, "It just ain't right." The truth of the matter is that the
world is broken and so are we.

Whether one calls it original sin or some sort of odd genetic moral
defect, we all must deal with recovery after our lives somehow have
been made miserable. We rail against suffering because imprinted
on our hearts is another way, a better way. The original intention for
human souls was not that we lead selfish, inward-looking lives,
which lead us to betray ourselves and those we love. It was for us to
walk in the garden with God, face-to-face.

One of the things that fascinate me about the Catholic Church is
that she squarely faces up to suffering and gives us myriad ways to
use it. I am a natural-born complainer, but the Church showed me
that there is a better way, as the prioress says, a more interesting
way. We may unite our suffering with Christ's as we "offer it up." We
may ask God to show us the good that he will bring from the evil we

are enduring. We may pray that with God's grace we may be molded a little more in the pattern of our Savior, who suffered much himself solely on our behalf. There is more than this little page can hold in the many ways that we may make our suffering into something greater. Let us grasp our opportunities with both hands and see how God uses everything we have to make us into someone greater too.

Dear Sir:

Regarding your article "What's Wrong with the World?" I am.

Yours truly,

G.K. Chesterton

. | . | . | . | . | .

Dusting Restoreth My Soul

> I suspected there was something important to be learned here....
> Mary seemed to approach housekeeping as an action, rather
> than a reaction. As she worked, it was clear that she was
> involved not in a process of negation (of dirt, dust, and the
> inevitable debris spawned by every activity of daily life) but of
> creation (of order, shiny surfaces, perfectly aligned towels, floors
> to which your feet did not stick). She seemed to have no doubt
> that what she was doing was important. She had faith, obvi-
> ously, in the restorative power of domesticity.
>
> Diane Schoemperlen, *Our Lady of the Lost and Found*

As positive as my attitude can be about many things, it is undeniable that the best I can muster is resignation when it comes to house-keeping. I don't think of how nice it will be to have order but rather of the work and time it takes. I think of the seemingly endless cycle that means I will never be done dusting. Never.

Housekeeping as an act of creation is such an important thing for me to remember. Is it silly to think of God creating order from chaos "in the beginning" and then realize that I am doing that very thing, albeit on an itty, bitty scale compared to him? Possibly. Still, silly is as silly does. An attitude of creation makes all the difference to the work I am doing and the pride I feel upon accomplishment. I can take being silly if it gets me that.

· | · | · | · | · | ·

Talk Like an Ordinary Person

One must have deeper motivations and judge everything accordingly, but still manage to talk like an ordinary person.

Attributed to Blaise Pascal

I didn't used to have this problem. Then I became Catholic. I'm not sure quite when it happened, but I'm fairly certain it was after I discovered theology books and began devouring them at an alarming rate.

Somehow my way of thinking and vocabulary were suddenly off kilter with the normal world. I found myself evaluating things differently but unable to discuss them easily with people who didn't belong to the same "club," if you will. There was a different vocabulary, a different set of standards against which formerly simple choices were judged.

For example, one of my daughters remarked one day on the way out of the grocery store, "So does that organization support abortion? Because I noticed you didn't give them a dollar at checkout and you used to." Embryonic stem cell research, but essentially she pegged it. I never would have cared or noticed before. Choices, always choices.

Yet one must be able to talk like an ordinary person, because otherwise how do you get across the ideas that have changed you so? How do you explain to others what has made such a difference and why it matters? It's a delicate balancing act but one that I might be getting better at thanks to all the practice. Believe me, there are plenty of opportunities for practice out there with all the normal people.

· | · | · | · | · | ·

An Absurd and Difficult Religion!

> What people don't realize is how much religion costs. They think faith is a big electric blanket, when of course it is the cross.
>
> Flannery O'Connor

That "church of the electric blanket" is exactly what I was taught growing up. More precisely put, there was the distinct impression that only the weak needed something like religion to help them get through life.

True enough, a Christian is never alone when in trouble and has God's grace to help get through life. However, after my conversion I discovered that the flip side to this is that we must always strive to walk in the Master's footsteps. Jesus has pretty big sandals to fill and a way of holding up perfection to be our guide. It is worth it, no doubt, but easy? No. Not really.

John C. Wright put it perfectly on his blog, fairly soon after he converted to Catholicism:

...[B]ut then you remember you are a Christian, and so you are under orders not merely not to complain (for even the Gentiles are well-bred) but to love and pray for such people? Worse yet, you cannot pray for them in an ungenerous spirit, because Our Boss who art in Heaven does not accept sacrifices offered unwillingly.

...This turn-the-other cheek jazz might be based on any number of psychological appeals or spiritual insights, but one thing it is not based on is wish fulfillment. An absurd and difficult religion! If it were not true, no one would bother with it.

Truth. Love.

The two reasons to follow, even unto the cross. Not easy, but well worth the cost.

. | • | • | • | • | •

None of My Business

I don't feel like it's any of my business what people think of me.

Jim Caviezel

As a faithful Catholic who is an actor, Jim Caviezel must have had to use that philosophy a lot to remain true to his faith. We all should take a lesson from his book and do likewise. I'm serious here. We really should.

I just want to ask though, has anyone else tried to practice what Jim Caviezel preaches?

I have. It is darned near impossible.

It was excruciating. It went completely against my nature. I like to win, especially when I've acted completely blamelessly, and I want everyone to like me. It is easy to talk about turning the other cheek, but doing it is far from easy.

I now have a completely new appreciation for Jesus not arguing with the tribunal, not striking down the soldiers who mocked him after the scourging, and humbly carrying that cross to his sacrificial death. He was blameless. But he let them think what they wanted. His reputation was in tatters long before that in all the "correct" circles.

My little tussle was nothing in comparison. Baby steps. Always baby steps.

> When someone strikes you on (your) right cheek, turn the other one to him as well.
>
> Matthew 5:39

• | • | • | • | • | •

The More Things Change, the More They Stay the Same

> Being involved intimately in a small parish means we are witness to everyone's foibles and failings and they get first-row seats to ours.... And sometimes the whole enterprise is discouraging. If we adults can't behave ourselves in a parish, of all places, where can we? Recently another thought has occurred to me: parish life is hard because life is hard. You don't get to pick your parents, and you don't get to pick who sits next to you in a pew.
>
> Alison, Why I Am Catholic blog

Indeed, yes. Sometimes we just simply disagree with each other because we all have perfectly legitimate positions that happen to be opposed to each other. It really does happen. Usually it gets ironed out. The trick is to do it with charity and good will. Oh, and not to be a sore loser if it doesn't go your way. These days that is really the toughest trick of all. Somehow we seem to feel empowered that if we are right, then we must win.

Sometimes, of course, the other person is simply wrong. (It could be me that is wrong, but really, how likely is that? Yep, that attitude is the whole problem in a nutshell.)

Ultimately I find this is eloquently summed up by a different quote from a computer programmer, because human nature is human nature, whether in or out of parish life.

> No matter how it looks at first, it's always a people problem.
>
> Gerald Weinberg

Ain't that the truth? It is quite ironic that a computer programmer who ostensibly has not got much to do with people has coined the perfect phrase to sum up the problem with community.

· | · | · | · | · | ·

Don't Do Me Any Favors Any More

> **Man on train:** Don't take that tone with me, young man. I fought the war for your sort.
> **Ringo:** I bet you're sorry you won.
>
> *A Hard Day's Night*

Have you ever done an act of charity for someone in such an ugly way that you might never be asked to do one again?

Haven't we all?

We feel ashamed even when we're doing it, but that doesn't stop us. Why not? Why do we give ourselves permission to behave badly? What does it take to make us stop for a second and think, shake our heads, and change right then?

Not later.

At that moment.

For me it means saying "no" firmly to the inner child who wants to get her own way. I need so much help to do that. However, there is nothing like the feeling when I pull it off.

Usually I'm glad later that I did.

OK. Truthfully?

I'm always glad later that I did.

Yet I fight that same fight repeatedly. That's the point though, isn't it? To keep fighting.

. | . | . | . | . | .

Choice and Consequences

Willard: I didn't have a choice!

Ned: Of course you did. Everything we do is a choice: oatmeal or cereal, highway or side street, kiss her or keep her. We make choices and we live with the consequences. If someone gets hurt along the way, we ask for forgiveness. It's the best anyone can do.

Pushing Daisies

That is a cry as old as time: "I didn't have a choice," when of course what is meant is "I didn't like the other choice!" We have given ourselves permission somehow to do what we want, and so often that just doesn't work out the way we wanted.

Usually we hear this when the "inevitable" choice that we so desired has gone bad somehow. It's funny how often that happens.

It is less satisfactory at the moment to make the hard choices.

34

Usually I wind up wishing I had done the right thing at the beginning. How many times am I going to have to learn that little lesson? Which, now that I think about it, is actually not a small lesson at all.

Rose Sayer: Human nature is what we were put on this earth to rise above.

The African Queen

. | . | . | . | . | .

Eye on the Prize

Tin Man: What have you learned, Dorothy?
Dorothy: Well, I…I think that it… it wasn't enough to just want to see Uncle Henry and Auntie Em, and it's that, if I ever go looking for my heart's desire again, I won't look any further than my own backyard. Because if it isn't there, I never really lost it to begin with! Is that right?

The Wizard of Oz

This moral lesson always seemed rather facile. Once again though, I look at this in the light of Christ and realize how much deeper it goes in terms of everyday life.

How often do I go looking in all the wrong places for what I think is my heart's desire? Later I find that I was wrong not only about where to look but about what my heart's desire was to begin with.

With practice I am getting better at looking inward in times of uncertainty or seeking. Praying. Slowing down. Keeping my eye on the ultimate prize.

The best thing is, it's taking fewer and fewer tornadoes and witches to get me to do it.

· | · | · | · | · | ·

Formatting Satan

> Satan will take the form of Excel spreadsheet cell G-14 this
> week and refuse to assume the proper formatting.
>
> *The Onion* horoscope

Elegantly done, eh? Poking fun at both horoscopes and Christians
who see the devil in every little thing that doesn't go their way.

I'm not saying that Satan isn't the prince of the world. The New
Testament assures us it is so. I'm not saying that he won't use whatever comes to hand. We know that is true. How better to tempt and
deceive than to just give a little twist to what is already there?

It does seem to me, though, that there are easier ways to do it.
Those ways usually involve making us love our fellowman less, trust
in God less, or both at once if possible. As a wise priest said to me
once, we usually don't need any help. We go astray often enough
under our own power not to need to see the devil behind every bush.
Or behind every spreadsheet cell.

· | · | · | · | · | ·

Victory in Surrender

> When we played a few [chess] matches, I learned what it is like
> to play against a master. Any classic offense I tried, he coun-
> tered with a classic defense. If I turned to more risky, unorthodox
> techniques, he incorporated my bold forays into his winning
> strategies. Even my apparent mistakes he worked to his advan-
> tage. I would gobble up an unprotected knight, only to discover

he had planted it there as a sacrificial lure, part of some grand
design.

Although I had complete freedom to make any move I
wished, I soon reached the conclusion that none of my strategies
mattered very much. His superior skill guaranteed that my pur-
poses inevitably ended up serving his own.... When a Grand
Master plays a chess amateur, victory is assured no matter how
the board may look at any given moment.

Philip Yancey

This is an eternal conundrum for mere mortals. How can God be
outside of time, all knowing, all-powerful, and yet still give us free
will? It hurts the head and has tested the minds of much better the-
ologians than I.

Philip Yancey's realization, as translated to the great adventure of
a life of faith, works for me on several levels. Not only does it help
me to grasp the mystery of God and our free will, but it speaks to
what I witnessed when my father was dying and suddenly, after a life
of antagonism toward God, simply changed. In giving in to the
inevitable fact of his impending death, he was forced to face eternity
and grasped God by the hand for those final days. How much sim-
pler and better life would have been if my father had done so from
the beginning.

Even so, we were privileged to see God's unrelenting quest to win
this match and not let his son, Keith, go alone into the dark. It was
an eye-opening lesson in free will and grand design from the Grand
Master.

· | · | · | · | · | ·

God Hung Among Thieves

The church is always God hung between two thieves. Thus, no one should be surprised or shocked at how badly the church has betrayed the gospel and how much it continues to do so today. It has never done very well. Conversely, however, nobody should deny the good the church has done either. It has carried grace, produced saints, morally challenged the planet, and made, however imperfectly, a house for God to dwell in on this earth.

To be connected with the church is to be associated with scoundrels, warmongers, fakes, child molesters, murderers, adulterers and hypocrites of every description. It also, at the same time, identifies you with saints and the finest persons of heroic soul within every time, country, race, and gender. To be a member of the church is to carry the mantle of both the worst sin and the finest heroism of soul...because the church always looks exactly as it looked at the original crucifixion, God hung among thieves.

Ronald Rolheiser

Some of us are scoundrels. Some of us are saints. Most of us are a complex blend of both in the middle. The Church transcends us all, while remaining mysteriously comprised of us all. It is only possible because Christ is in our midst.

Thanks be to God.

· | · | · | · | · | ·

The Times They Are a-Changing, But We Are an Old, Old Story

Men will surrender to the spirit of the age. They will say that if
they had lived in our day, faith would be simple and easy. But
in their day, they will say, things are complex; the Church
must be brought up to date and made meaningful to the day's
problems.

St. Anthony of the Desert (fourth century)

How much proof do we need that human nature is unchanging?

I read the Old Testament with all the ancient stories. Even minor
details shout out behavior that we all recognize. Joseph's bratty
teenaged bragging, Onan's stubborn refusal to do his duty by his
brother's widow while taking his pleasure, Enoch's longing for his
mother's love, and so many more characters cry out with sheer
humanity. Four thousand years later I understand them.

I read the New Testament and think of how much Dallasites have
in common with the wealthy Corinthians Paul scolded, how none of
us keep secrets, just like the leper who told everyone about his healing instead of keeping quiet as Jesus commanded, how Peter's habit
of speaking up so often showed his lack of thought. Braggarts,
cheats, misers, we meet them all near Jesus. Two thousand years
later I understand them.

I read the writings from the fathers of the Church (in a wonderful book by Mike Aquilina). They exhorted the faithful and each
other, battled over the nature of God and the Church, and encour-
aged their flocks in living every day as Christians. I read about the
saints, all finding their own paths to God, all created to shine his

light in the way that their own times needed most, all struggling to overcome their own "self." Arguing, scolding, pleading, loving. Thousands of years later, hundreds of years later, yesterday, and today. I understand them.

The times they always are a-changing. But we, we stay the same.

· | · | · | · | · | ·

Much Depends on Dinner

> The dinner table is the center for the teaching and practicing not just of table manners but of conversation, consideration, tolerance, family feeling, and just about all the other accomplishments of polite society except the minuet.
>
> *Miss Manners' Guide for the Turn-of-the-Millennium*

> Things come up when you sit down together and there are fewer distractions. I'm glad I was at the table the night our seven-year-old son asked, "If they found the lost city of Atlantis, how many electoral votes would it have?"...If you don't eat together, you don't hear this stuff.
>
> Bonny Wolf

Without family meals together, we would never have had spirited debates about such mysteries as a goldfish's memory span. What is the test given to a goldfish to see if it really is only five seconds? How about that fact put on the board by the science teacher who said that a duck's quack doesn't echo? These are the times that made us long for an encyclopedia instead of the dictionary and eventual stack of other reference books that lived for a time on our sideboard, handy for quick fact-checking.

You can see that I am a firm believer that the family that dines together thrives together. Even when the times are sad or mad instead of glad. Much depends on dinner conversation, and all the unexpected moments that go along with it. Those are the moments that live on in memory as well as influence the moment

. | . | . | . | . | .

Talk Is Cheap

> Humanly speaking, it is possible to understand the Sermon on the Mount in a thousand different ways. But Jesus knows only one possibility: simple surrender and obedience—not interpreting or applying it, but doing and obeying it. That is the only way to hear his words. He does not mean for us to discuss it as an ideal. He really means for us to get on with it.
>
> Dietrich Bonhoeffer

Doing and obeying may be some of the most difficult work we ever do. Struggling with our wills is a never-ending battle. We win on one front only to discover that we've slipped somewhere else. But the victory. Oh, the victory is a glorious moment of union with God.

I do not experience it often.

I'm no more perfect than anyone else.

But I savor it when I do.

· | · | · | · | · | ·

Looking Past the Tangles

> There's a woman who is embroidering. Her son, seated on a
> low stool, sees her work, but in reverse. He sees the knots of the
> embroidery, the tangled threads. He says, "Mother, what are
> you doing? I can't make out what you are doing!" Then the
> mother lowers the embroidery hoop and shows the good part
> of the work. Each color is in place, and the various threads form
> a harmonious design. So, we see the reverse side of the embroi-
> dery because we are seated on the low stool.
>
> St. Pio

I just love this guy, an Italian priest who knew how to throw his head
back and laugh, who would scold a famous actress for being shallow,
who suffered the stigmata for over fifty years, who knew (and could
see) his guardian angel from the time he was a tiny child, who could
bilocate (appear in two places at once) and read souls, who was one
of the greatest saints in living memory...and with whom I share a
birth date (although his was seventy years earlier).

I first "met" St. Pio while leafing through a book of modern
saints' photos. He was laughing with his head thrown back, commu-
nicating a sense of joy and lightheartedness. I thought, "Now, *there*
is someone I could talk to.... That is what a real saint should look
like."

That photo exemplified the principle in his quote. If you read
about St. Pio, you might get the idea that his life was nothing but
suffering. However, looking at that photo showed me someone who
lived with gusto.

The big picture. We have to keep it in mind when the knots and
tangles are getting us down.

· | · | · | · | · | ·

Why Do You Think They Call It Will*power*, Old Chum?

Robin: Self-control is sure tough sometimes, Batman!

Batman: All virtues are, old chum. Indeed, that's why they're virtues.

Batman TV series

We have a shaky understanding of the virtues these days, perhaps because they require self-control to practice, and self-control has gone out of style. The great thing about the virtues, however, is that they are the perfect opportunity to instill habits so that we don't have to fight temptation every single time. Our will is like a muscle. If it isn't exercised, then it gets flabby and can't do the job it is meant to do. I like exercising willpower just about as much as I like jogging, which is to say, not at all. However, I have found that it doesn't take much self-denial to notice a difference in how much easier it becomes to turn aside from temptation. And that feels pretty good.

What are the virtues? Glad you asked. As defined by the Church fathers they are prudence, justice, restraint (or temperance), courage (or fortitude), faith, hope, and love (or charity). I don't have room to talk about them here, but it is worth seeking out descriptions to consider how to work them into our lives more fully.

I believe Batman, after all. They're tough. But worth it.

• | • | • | • | • | •

Quirky Is as Quirky Does

"You have some queer* friends, Dorothy," she said.
"The queerness doesn't matter, so long as they're friends,"
was the answer.

L. Frank Baum, *The Road to Oz*

We all have some quirks, and don't they make us just that much
more lovable? Well, don't my quirks do so?

Sometimes.

I have to admit that the quirkier friends are the ones that try my
patience more. What a bland world it would be though without those
quirks. They're like a needed dash of salt on a plate of boiled rice.
Not only do those friends keep me on my toes and enrich my life,
but they kindly overlook my quirks. For which I am grateful.

---

* This was written in 1909, when the word queer meant "eccentric" or
"unconventional."

• | • | • | • | • | •

Pied Beauty

Glory be to God for dappled things—
For skies of couple-colour as a brinded cow;
For rose-moles all in stipple upon trout that swim;
Fresh-firecoal chestnut-falls; finches' wings;
Landscape plotted and pieced—fold, fallow, and plough;
And all trades, their gear and tackle and trim.
All things counter, original, spare, strange;

Whatever is fickle, freckled (who knows how?)
With swift, slow; sweet, sour; adazzle, dim;
He fathers-forth whose beauty is past change:
Praise him.

Gerard Manley Hopkins

My mother's love of nature poured onto us as children. We "rescued" turtles, watched a black snake try repeatedly to eat an egg too big for its mouth, knew spring was coming when the red-winged blackbirds returned to our little pond each year.

I am not very fond of poetry, but this takes me back to those days. It makes me look with new eyes at the world around us—the world of beauty that God created for us to delight in. It says something about his nature and our own creation in his image. It makes me step away from my computer and go into the backyard where, above the traffic whizzing by, I can hear a mockingbird singing, see the pear blossoms lushly white against a vivid blue sky, feel the cool breeze in my hair, and marvel at the mind that created all this beauty. It is so different from anything we would have thought up if we'd have been in charge of creation.

Praise him.

· | · | · | · | · | ·

Loving Not Wisely But Too Well

I have never understood people who want to keep their children as babies and regret every year that they grow older. I myself sometimes felt that I could hardly wait; I wanted to see exactly what Rosalind would be like in a year's time, a year after that, and so on. There is nothing more thrilling in this world, I think, than having a child that is yours, and yet is mysteriously a stranger. You are the gate through which it came into the world, and you will be allowed to have charge of it for a period; after that it will leave you and blossom out into its own free life , and there it is, for you to watch, living its life in freedom. It is like a strange plant which you have brought home, planted, and can hardly wait to see how it will turn out.

Agatha Christie, *An Autobiography*

I admire the clarity of thought that rises above our sheer love for our children and enables us to see that a child is a unique creature who isn't a reflection of ourselves.

One of the benefits of having your house be the one where the kids are all welcome to hang out is that you become the recipient of many confidences. So often I have heard of parents trying to mold their children into someone completely opposite to their personalities. It's rather ironic, considering that these parents often are some of the proudest over raising their children to think for themselves. What they cannot recognize is that they have achieved their goal. In raising their children to be independent thinkers, they inadvertently raised people who do not necessarily agree with them.

What hurts equally is that the children often recognize this and try to tolerate it for their parents' sakes but simply cannot because they would be smothered. They recognize the efforts at control as gestures of love, even as on a practical level they almost desperately rebel in order to survive. My heart aches for them all, the children and the parents.

How much better it is to be able to eagerly anticipate the exotic beauties that surprise you at every turn.

· | · | · | · | · | ·

Manners Make the Man

Brian: There's no pleasing some people.

Ex-leper: That's what Jesus said.

Life of Brian

The *Life of Brian* mocks religious hypocrisy. A lot of people protested the movie when it came out, thinking that it was mocking Christ. No. Monty Python didn't have to reach that high. We Christians provide a much easier target. And the worst part is that our critics are not really wrong.

In fact, it might have surprised Monty Python, but the movie often parallels many of the truths Jesus taught. He also was good at mocking hypocrites, as many a Pharisee knew to his chagrin.

When it comes to being ungrateful for Jesus' healing, we have a prime example in John 5:1–16. Jesus heals a crippled man who has spent thirty-eight years trying to get into the pool when the angel's wing touched it so he could be healed. The man's reaction? When Jesus tells him that he should sin no more, he goes to Jesus' persecutors, who had been sniffing around for dirt about Jesus healing on the Sabbath, and turns him in. Ouch!

However, John (9:1–41) also gives us the converse of that with the blind man who will not condemn Jesus when the Pharisees push him to do so. In fact, he goes further. He defends Jesus to the Pharisees at some risk to himself:

> The man answered and said to them, "This is what is so amaz-
> ing, that you do not know where he is from, yet he opened my
> eyes. We know that God does not listen to sinners, but if one

is devout and does his will, he listens to him. It is unheard of that anyone ever opened the eyes of a person born blind. If this man were not from God, he would not be able to do anything." They answered and said to him, "You were born totally in sin, and are you trying to teach us?" Then they threw him out.

John 9:30–34

We face this dilemma every time we hesitate in a conversation in which our Christianity comes up. These days that's probably more than any of us care to admit. The choice is always to condemn or defend, for narrowness or openness, for limitations or freedom. Which do we choose?

· | · | · | · | · | ·

Angels, Vampires, and Heroes

> **Angel:** Nothing in the world is the way it ought to be, Connor. It's harsh, and cruel. But that's why there's us. Champions. It doesn't matter where we come from, what we've done or suffered, or even if we make a difference. We live as though the world was what it should be, to show it what it can be.
>
> *Angel*

Champions? Or saints?

For a self-proclaimed atheist, Joss Whedon manages to pack a lot of Christian concepts into his television shows and movies. Perhaps it is because Whedon is clearly in love with the art of storytelling at its very best, which means that it shows us a hero. Vampires, monsters, and rebels in a sci-fi future are among Whedon's protagonists. All have at their heart a concept that there is a higher ideal we should be living. Even when they fall short, they get back up and try again. They never lower their standards. They never stop trying to reach that goal.

Sounds like the definition of a saint to me.

. | . | . | . | . | .

Early Birds and Worms

> God gives every bird his worm, but He does not throw it into the nest.
>
> P.D. James

We were each created for a purpose. I can guarantee that purpose requires us to do our utmost in whatever we are called to do, whether by simple everyday living or if we suspect a higher purpose at work.

I don't know about you, but I do know a few folks who will prayerfully bring some need to God and then sit back and wait for the answer to drop into their laps. This approach always takes me aback somewhat, for all the saints I ever read about worked their fingers to the bone to achieve God's desires. Why are we here if not to serve and work as best we can?

Surely St. Augustine, arguably the greatest doctor of the Church and the writer to whom is given much of the credit for the basis of Western philosophical thinking, must have thought so. He certainly mentions it more than once, though not quite as colorfully as above. He is credited with saying: "Pray as though everything depended on God. Work as though everything depended on you."

· | · | · | · | · | ·

Hold On, I Know I've Got a Quarter Here

God is not a vending machine.

Joan Kimber

So all the people took off their earrings and brought them to Aaron, who accepted their offering, and fashioning this gold with a graving tool, made a molten calf. Then they cried out, "This is your God, O Israel, who brought you out of the land of Egypt" (Exodus 32:3–4).

The reason the Hebrews demanded a golden calf is largely misunderstood these days. It was not to worship the statue. They wanted to summon him at will to answer their prayers.

It is convenient to look back over the chasm of time, shaking our heads sadly at these willful people. They had Moses in their midst, God's own choice, and they still tried to get their own way.

We would do better to look in the mirror than to "tut-tut" over the Hebrews. We are no better. We don't want to suffer, we know just how to solve this problem if he'd just listen to our prayers, and, Lord Almighty, do hurry up, because we surely don't want to wait around!

How limiting this is. It narrows our vision and our recognition of God's plan, which is so much broader than anything we can possibly know. Not only that, we are cutting ourselves off from the surprises he has planned. Those of us who have had any glimpse of the divine plan know that we never would have thought of anything like God's intricate, elegant, multilayered design.

We would do far better to follow the Car Guys' wise advice: "Don't tell the mechanic what to fix. Just tell him the problem, and let him come up with the solution."

That he knows it is enough.

. | . | . | . | . | .

Scuba Diving

> Human beings are very much like icebergs—we only see a
> small portion of them, and nothing of the hidden currents which
> drag them this way and that.
>
> I fancy that we would not sit and judge our neighbor so fre-
> quently as we do, did we but ponder well over the small amount
> of data we possess. We perceive only the external act, but noth-
> ing of the motive activating it.
>
> Fr. David McAstocker

If the guy sitting next to me at Mass isn't singing, it tips my radar.
Maybe he isn't Catholic? No, he just crossed himself, and he knew
what he was doing. No hesitancy.

Maybe he was dragged here by his family? No, he's distinctly different from the people on the other side of him in the pew.

So, he's not singing because he's a slacker. Yep. Mystery solved.

At this point I usually remember I'm not here to function as the
Mass police. I'm here to worship, and a mighty poor job I'm doing
of it with all my attention on that non-singer. As my husband likes
to point out, "We tend to judge others by their actions, but we want
to be judged by our intentions."

Ahem.

Perhaps that poor fellow has a sore throat. I'd better say a prayer
for him. Also for myself.

· | · | · | · | · | ·

Fear Not the TV

Homer Simpson: Television—teacher, mother, secret lover.

The Simpsons

In high school I spent a formative year or two with my best friend's family trying out their Protestant church. It was what might be labeled rather fundamentalist. They didn't drink and wouldn't even have wine for cooking in their cupboard; they didn't play cards; they didn't go to movies. They did, however, watch television, despite the fact that, like all those other activities, it exposed their souls to great danger.

On the other hand, I could make my father a manhattan by the time I was twelve, our grandparents had taught us to play bridge by the age of nine, and we adored movies. We also watched television. So at least there was one thing in common with the church members.

What was puzzling was why everyone felt so threatened by such apparently mundane activities? Did they not trust themselves? Did they not trust God?

It would be easy to say it's a Protestant problem. Or a Muslim problem. Anything except a Catholic problem. Truth is though that you run into the same mind-set in every sort of group. For some reason there is a whiff of paranoia that makes people want to limit access to perfectly legitimate activities because they feel they can't trust themselves around them. Or trust others to behave properly either.

Thank goodness the Church trusts me to search my heart for what is right in this matter. This is the freedom that God gives. Free will.

· | · | · | · | · | ·

Lenty-ness

Oh, Lent. It never fails to be Lenty.

Mamacita at The Summa Mamas blog

Lent is a snapshot of the process we go through our whole lives. It is about pushing aside the peripherals to reach the alignment of our lives, our wills, our selves with the will of the Father. It is like boot camp in a way.

Fr. John Libone

I do not look forward to Lent, specifically because it is so "Lenty." We are taken into the desert. It is difficult there, spare and unrelenting. But there is a sort of peace and beauty that comes from having your soul scoured clean by the whirling sands.

In a strange way I am grateful for that scouring. If I reach the eye of the storm, there can be such peace in having to throw myself on God's grace. I realize how very imperfect I am. I realize just how superhuman, how supernatural it was for Christ to undergo what he did in his passion and to do it so perfectly. I realize how grateful I am that we have his example, simultaneously perfectly human and perfectly divine, to follow and not only that of our fellowmen, imperfect as we all are.

Is it peaceful here because it is real, because we can see so clearly when stripped away from the extraneous trees and landscape of regular life? I do not know. I do know that I feel an understanding of the desert saints that I never have before.

We are not meant to "succeed" at Lent but to fail and know our dependence upon Grace.

Elizabeth Scalia

· | · | · | · | · | ·

A Little Donkey

> When I am paid a compliment, I must compare myself with the little donkey that carried Christ on Palm Sunday. And I say to myself: If that little creature, hearing the applause of the crowd, had become proud and had begun—jackass that he was—to bow his thanks right and left like a prima donna, how much hilarity he would have aroused! Don't act the same!
>
> Cardinal Luciani (later Pope John Paul I)

We all have something that we are good at. The question is, do we recognize the source of the gifts we possess? Hopefully we use them well, strive to do our best, and achieve much. Often this leads to attention and to compliments. We may take some credit, to be sure, but how much more is due to the bestower of the innate abilities we use, the true source of all good things?

The root of true humility is to be able to clearly assess the good and the bad and see the source of each. I have my "little donkey" moments. However, I am actually getting better at having my Einstein moments as well. Now, that's progress.

> For the most part I do what my own nature drives me to do. It is embarrassing to earn such respect and love for it.
>
> Albert Einstein

· | · | · | · | · | ·

Soufflés and Ballets

Noncooks think it's silly to invest two hours' work in two minutes' enjoyment; but if cooking is evanescent, so is the ballet.

Julia Child

We live in an age that increasingly values the tangible, the concrete, the measurable over anything else. Yet the things that make life worth living can be the most fleeting and intangible.

Every example I can think of is a cliché: a bird singing, fireworks bursting in the dark sky, a glorious sunset, my daughters' smiles, my husband's arms around me. Clichés are clichés, after all, because they are so universal. They are truths that everyone recognizes.

Tangible but real. Like prayers. Like love. Like God.

We know it is there. We feel it.

Even when it is as simple as a soufflé.

· | · | · | · | · | ·

A Little Knowledge Is a Dangerous Thing

He laughed, "Is it true that in America, if you die of old age, it's your fault?"

I nodded gravely, "You should have jogged more. Or not smoked, or checked your cholesterol, or abstained from the juice."

"And then what?"

"And then you exist miserably for years with tubes."

Dick Francis, Wild Horses

You don't really expect to find such an accurate and merciless assessment of American character in the middle of a mystery novel. It made me laugh. It made me think.

What is it about Americans that we take our can-do spirit and turn it into an unrealistic obsession with conquering everything, including elements that a sensible person knows are clearly outside any person's control? Then, just for good measure, we feel guilty about it because failing means we didn't do it right.

I remember the days when one either enjoyed taking a stroll or didn't. It wasn't put down to being a slacker about fitness. That was just what one enjoyed. Or didn't.

When did even such simple things as going to the grocery store become fraught with emotional tension? Bananas? Wait, what about the damage done to the environment in transporting them?

I find myself very tired of the moral high ground.

I am suddenly nostalgic for the good old days when you could smoke a cigarette, have a burger, or sip a cocktail without fear of getting a dirty look.

·　　|　　·　　|　　·　　|　　·　　|　　·　　|　　·

The Hinge Upon Which All Else Depends

Happy families are all alike; every unhappy family is unhappy in its own way.

Leo Tolstoy, *Anna Karenina*

From where I sit, Tolstoy got it half right. The more I see of life, and especially with the prayer requests I hear, I begin to realize that happy and unhappy families move upon the same hinge.

Each is the result of the need for sacrifice and love to mingle and be given to the others at the expense of the individual. Happy families serve each other and promote that idea. Unhappy families have at least one person who consistently puts his or her own desires before those of anyone else. The unhappiness is acted out in myriad fashions by the family members, but the cause is the same. This surely has been my own experience in both sorts of families, growing up and now as an adult.

It is easier then to see why God made the family the cornerstone of society and, indeed, of our lives. It is here that we learn how to give to others before ourselves and how to depend upon each other in times when we can't do it alone.

> To maintain a joyful family requires much from both the parents and the children. Each member of the family has to become, in a special way, the servant of the others.
>
> Pope John Paul II

· | · | · | · | · | ·

Let God Come Walking Through

> But if a show is a little off, and there's a hole, that's the one song we can guarantee that God will walk through the room as soon as we play it. So the idea that when we played it, people would go, "That's the such-and-such commercial," we couldn't live with it.
>
> Bono, on why U2 refused £12.5 million for commercial use of "Where the Streets Have No Name"

I'm not a fan of U2's music. I'm not a fan of all Bono's causes.

But I know integrity and honesty when I see it.

So, yeah.

I'm a fan.

. | . | . | . | . | .

Does God Grade on the Curve?

> I'm not all that much of a praying person, and I'm definitely not
> a religious person, but I do consider myself a spiritual person
> and a Christian. I guess I might be a C-minus Christian, but I am
> one.
>
> Johnny Cash

I think about what that statement means in terms of what I know
about Johnny Cash's life: suffering, fighting personal demons,
hurting those he loved most, and always getting back up to keep trying again. I think that a lot of the time what we deem Christian and
what God deems Christian can be two very different things.

That's possibly why we shouldn't be so quick to grade each other.
Very possibly it may be why, in the end, we don't get to grade ourselves.

. | . | . | . | . | .

Look, Dear, Another Second-Rate Turner Tonight

> Nobody of any real culture, for instance, ever talks nowadays
> about the beauty of a sunset. Sunsets are quite old-fashioned.
> They belong to the time when Turner was the last note in art. To

admire them is a distinct sign of provincialism of temperament. Upon the other hand they go on. Yesterday evening Mrs. Arundel insisted on my going to the window, and looking at the glorious sky, as she called it. Of course I had to look at it. She is one of those absurdly pretty Philistines to whom one can deny nothing. And what was it? It was simply a very second-rate Turner, a Turner of a bad period, with all the painter's worst faults exaggerated and over-emphasised.

Oscar Wilde

God's art can have a flamboyant style, no doubt about it.

Sometimes I am struck by the fact that the very bit of nature I am enjoying would make a painting so garish that I wouldn't hang it on my own wall. Maybe it's because the medium is different—paint and canvas instead of air, wind, scent, light, sound, movement, life. Always the same, always changing. What media, what a master artist.

I've got to admit we could do worse than to look for reflections of the artist in his masterpieces. Perhaps tonight, while standing outside admiring the second-rate Turner presented for our enjoyment?

. | . | . | . | . | .

Be Not Afraid

How to defeat terrorism? Don't be terrorized. Don't let fear rule your life. Even if you are scared.

Salman Rushdie

We do not pretend that life is all beauty. We are aware of darkness and sin, of poverty and pain. But we know Jesus has conquered sin and passed through his own pain to the glory of the Resurrection. And we live in the light of his paschal mystery—the mystery of his death and resurrection.

Pope John Paul II

Two men with the same message. Both very different. Yet both have suffered from tyrannies trying to silence what is true. Pope John Paul II in Poland endured first under the Nazis and then under the communist regime. Salman Rushdie was sent into hiding after having a fatwa (death sentence) pronounced on him by certain Islamic religious leaders because of his book *The Satanic Verses*.

These men clearly had reasons to be afraid, and yet both persevered.

It is easy to be fearful. I see the evidence in media where item after item is discussed whose only result seems to be to make people I know worry. I read recently that we may be the most fearful generation ever, despite having more luxuries and safety than any people before us.

Is it because we know too much? Is it because we do not trust Christ enough?

I recall my brother talking about how natural it is to be afraid of dying. In the next breath he stunned me by saying, "But all that would do is take me home. I'm a Christian. Should I be afraid of that? No."

A good reminder and reorientation for me. Perhaps for us all. Where does our hope lie?

Be not afraid.

· | · | · | · | · | ·

Losing for Love

> **Jocelyn:** Instead of winning to honor me with your high reputa-
> tion, I want you to act against your normal character and do
> badly. Lose!
> **William:** Losing proves nothing, except that I'm a loser.
> **Jocelyn:** Wrong! Losing is a much keener test of your love.
> Losing would contradict your self-love, and losing would show
> your obedience to your lover and not to yourself!
> **William:** No!
> **Jocelyn:** What is your answer?
> **William:** I will not lose.
> **Jocelyn:** Then you do not love me.
>
> *A Knight's Tale*

It's a funny thing to be watching a B movie and suddenly be hit by
the Christlike nature of the sacrifice the girl is asking of her suitor.
A Knight's Tale seems on the surface to be merely a fun movie. And
yet...

We do not have to scratch far below the surface of clever pop culture references intertwined with a tale set long ago to see that we are
being shown a young man who has higher goals than most. He wants
to be a knight, but he also properly understands that to be a knight
is to be honorable. Problematically, he still has something to learn
of what real honor is. Jocelyn's demand goes against what he naturally desires, and yet, in order to show his love, he must sacrifice
himself in a way that few would understand.

Watching William sit there, not even raising a lance in his own defense in order to prove his love to Jocelyn, made me think of the ultimate hero, the one who taught us what honor really is, who sacrificed all to show us his love and save us from the consequences of our own pride.

> For Jews demand signs and Greeks look for wisdom, but we proclaim Christ crucified, a stumbling block to Jews and foolishness to Gentiles, but to those who are called, Jews and Greeks alike, Christ the power of God and the wisdom of God. For the foolishness of God is wiser than human wisdom, and the weakness of God is stronger than human strength.
>
> 1 Corinthians 1:22–25

· | · | · | · | · | ·

We Wasn't Born to Be All the Time Scared

"You're a very brave young man, Jacob Calvino" [said Odd Thomas].

"She said...she said don't be scared, we wasn't born to be all the time scared, we was born happy, babies laugh at everything, we was born happy and to make a better world."

"I wish I'd known your mother."

"She said everyone...everyone, if he's rich or he's poor, if he's somebody big or nobody at all—everyone has a grace." A look of peace came over his embattled face when he said the word grace. "You know what a grace is?"

"Yes."

"A grace is a thing you get from God, you use it to make a better world, or not use it, you have to choose."

"Like your art" [Odd Thomas] said. "Like your beautiful draw-
ings."

He said, "Like your pancakes."

"Ah, you know I made those pancakes, huh?"

"Those pancakes, that's a grace."

Dean Koontz, *Brother Odd*

I was fairly stunned to come across such a down-to-earth discussion of God's grace in a horror book. Dean Koontz, however, is a
Catholic who is growing deeply in his faith, if his recent books are
any indication.

When I hear people lamenting the fact that there aren't any Catholic
authors anymore, like Flannery O'Connor, Percy Walker, and
Graham Greene, the author who comes to my mind is Dean Koontz.
He is one of those authors who I think people will look back at in the
future as part of the "new school" of Catholic authors. Just as
O'Connor, Walker, and Greene expressed their Catholic faith natu-
rally in the fiction they wrote, we see authors like Dean Koontz,
Michael Flynn, and Tim Powers doing the same.

They are prime examples of how you can communicate faith,
truth, and hope in the unlikeliest ways, even to those who don't
know what they're absorbing. These authors do this simply by writing the best darned stories they can, and along the way their worldview naturally forms part of the logic they use.

There is much more than just an exciting story in a Koontz novel
for those who have eyes to see. Many would not enjoy a horror novel,
even knowing that a deeper message lies between the lines. I myself
eschew some things that doubtless also have truths waiting below
the surface.

I suppose that is why God has graces surrounding us in all the people we encounter. Even when all they are doing is making but-termilk pancakes.

· | · | · | · | · | ·

That Movie Moment

Cast your bread upon the waters; after a long time you may find it again.

Ecclesiastes 11:1

Don't ask yourself what the world needs. Ask yourself what makes you come alive, and go do it. Because what the world needs is people who have come alive.

Dr. Howard Thurman

When I was considering beginning a blog, my husband was all for it. Years later, when I was considering a podcast, my husband was all for it. (What a guy!)

Recently I apologized for all the time these projects took, for the inconvenience they had caused him in the toll of skimpy dinners, little housework, and less hours at work in our business together.

He said, "Yes, sometimes it was inconvenient and even annoying. But I saw the blog as one of those movie moments, those events that change everything. I could have complained, but I knew that would change it for you. And I wanted you to have that movie moment if it was there."

I had no idea. What a tribute. What a gift of sheer love. What a man. How blessed I am that God thought I could live up to having a husband like that.

My husband's willing gift allowed me to come more alive, to cast my bread upon the waters, and led to things I never would have imagined. Truly a movie moment on many levels.

·　|　·　|　·　|　·　|　·　|　·

Shining Like the Sun

> In the center of the shopping district, I was suddenly overwhelmed with the realization that I loved all those people, that they were mine and I theirs, that we could not be alien to one another even though we were total strangers.... There is no way of telling people that they are all walking around shining like the sun.... It is so to speak his name written in us.... It is in everybody, and if we could see it we would see these billions of points of light coming together in the face and blaze of a sun that would make all the darkness and cruelty of life vanish completely.... [T]he gate of heaven is everywhere.
>
> Thomas Merton, *Conjectures of a Guilty Bystander*

> I saw no temple in the city, for its temple is the Lord God almighty and the Lamb. The city had no need of sun or moon to shine on it, for the glory of God gave it light, and its lamp was the Lamb.
>
> Revelation 21:22–23

The book of Revelation was written to bring light and hope during a dark time for Christianity. Like all the rest of the Bible, of course, it also applies to our own journey through life. John is talking about heaven. He is also talking about our lives, whether or not he knew it when he was writing. That is part of the mystery with which the Holy Spirit inspired the writers of Holy Scripture.

What Thomas Merton saw was what John saw when he was writing Revelation. Different times, different ways to express it. Jesus, the Lamb of God, Emmanuel, God with us, is with us everywhere and always. Giving us light, warming our souls.

Kneeling, watching the halting parade of people coming for Communion, old couples clinging to each other shuffling by, tiny children waving over their parents' shoulders at us in the pews, five little boys who came to Mass dressed for soccer, slouching teenagers in sweatshirts and jeans, I think of how we all shine like the sun. I think of the city in Revelation with no temple, no need for light because God is everywhere.

All of us called by God. All responding in our own way. All shining like the sun. And I love them.

· | · | · | · | · | ·

Is Your Battery Charged?

"You think Mother sent us out here [into the wilderness with no supplies] to have visions?" Ralph asked.

"Maybe to gain strength and holiness by a purging process," Glen said. "The casting away of things is symbolic, you know. Talismanic. When you cast away things, you're also casting away the self-related others that are symbolically related to those things. You start a cleaning-out process. You begin to empty the vessel."

Larry shook his head slowly. "I don't follow that."...

"Now think of yourself as a battery. You really are, you know. Your brain runs on chemically converted electrical current.... Okay. The point is this: Everything you think, everything you do, it all has to run off the battery. Like the accessories in a car."

They were all still listening closely.

"Watching TV, reading books, talking with friends, eating a big dinner...all of it runs off the battery. A normal life—at least in what used to be Western civilization—was like running a car with power windows, power brakes, power seats, all the good- ies. But the more goodies you have, the less the battery can charge. True?"

"Yeah," Ralph said. "Even a big Delco won't ever overcharge when it's sitting in a Cadillac."

"Well, what we've done is to strip off the accessories. We're on charge."

Stephen King, *The Stand*

Is my battery charged?

Not enough.

I just might not wait until Lent to give something up and let God enter in.

· | · | · | · | · | ·

Chaucer Didn't Have Any Idea, and Neither Do I

I took a course in college on Chaucer, one of the most explo- sive, imaginative, and far-reaching in influence on all writers. And I'll never forget going to the final exam and being asked why Chaucer used certain verbal devices, certain objectives, why he had certain characters behave in certain ways. And I wrote in a white heat of fury, "I don't think Chaucer had any idea why he did any of these things. That isn't the way people write."

> I believe this as strongly now as I did then. Most of what is
> best in writing isn't done deliberately.
>
> Madeleine L'Engle

One has only to think of it from this angle to see how odd it actually is to tear apart writing for verbal devices and such things. Can you imagine writing a book using those constructs as your guides? Or to put it another way, I suppose that one could write a book that way, but it would read like something a computer turned out. It would definitely be lacking in honest passion, intuition, feelings... humanity.

Art—and writing is art—comes from the heart. If you have read enough and widely enough, you will have a sense of how words and sentences and paragraphs and, above all, stories should come together. You may not be able to analyze it. But you could write it. From the heart.

· | · | · | · | · | ·

Intertwined Moments

> All unhappiness, as you live with it, becomes shot through with
> happiness; it cannot help it; and all happiness, I suppose, is shot
> through with unhappiness.
>
> Rumer Godden, *China Court*

What is it in our natures that makes us want everything to be all one way or the other? The truth is that life just doesn't work that way. Life is a messy mystery.

We're the same. People are a mystifying combination of good and bad that we don't even recognize in ourselves. Chalk it up to original sin, or call it some psychological term. It's just human nature.

It is this that gives us our feet of clay. Why are we continually surprised by it? Perhaps because deep in our hearts we know that this
isn't how things originally were intended to be. We strive unknow-
ingly for that divine goal, and it just can't be achieved here on earth.

There are moments, of course, heavenly moments of rightness,
but they are usually shot through with earthly moments of wrong-
ness. Just as Rumer Godden reminds us.

· | · | · | · | · | ·

A Simple Artist's Prayer

> **Dewey:** God of Rock, thank you for this chance to kick a**.
> We are your humble servants. Please give us the power to blow
> people's minds with our high-voltage rock. In your name we
> pray, Amen.
>
> *School of Rock*

A simple prayer, honestly offered. I like to think that Jesus grants
prayers like that. Especially to those who have worked their hardest
to show truth in their art, whatever it may be.

Yes, it is a joke in a movie. A movie that is a paean to rock and roll.

It is nevertheless true for all that. Truth is where we find it,
regardless of the source. Whether Christian or not, whether about
God or not. If God is Truth, then he is where we find him, however
small the splinter may be. Who are we to turn away from it?

> For a Christian to say, "I will not have anything to do with the
> great and worthy works of artists whose lives were not good,"
> is to fall into the impiety of questioning the wisdom of God in
> bestowing gifts of grace where He wills.
>
> Frank Gaebelein

· | · | · | · | · | ·

Mise en place*

> For if you do not understand a man, you cannot crush him. And
> if you do understand him, very probably you will not.
>
> G.K. Chesterton, "Humanitarianism and Strength"

It seems odd to think about studying someone so that we could crush him. Let's be honest though. At times people are so annoying that we do indeed wish to crush them, if only to shut them up. It is most likely to be verbal combat, but the principle holds true. If you disagree with someone, you must know the ins and outs of your opponent's arguments better than they do themselves. Your goal is to shut them down so they must admit the strength of your arguments and that you are right. It is called winning. Decisively.

There is nothing wrong with winning or even preparing to thoroughly defeat someone. However, one must proceed with caution, because with understanding comes minds opening to new ideas, possibly even to the reason that your opponent is so adamantly against your point of view. You may not change your mind, but I practically guarantee that it will change how you view the person you are opposing.

That can't be anything but good.

---

*French phrase for having everything prepared and in place for cooking.

· | · | · | · | · | ·

You Ain't So Smart

> "And I'll tell you another thing, Hulga," he said, using the name
> as if he didn't think much of it, "you ain't so smart. I been believ-
> ing in nothing ever since I was born."
>
> Flannery O'Connor, "Good Country People"

It was not until I read this story that I was struck hard by a very basic
fact. It is not difficult to believe in only what you can see, feel, and
prove. Why then do outspoken atheists and secular humanists act as
if they are revolutionary free thinkers for doing so? A baby thinks
that if Mother has gone round the corner, then she has disappeared.
An adult knows that she is simply out of sight but still near at hand.

What is truly risky is to look for truth in places that are less tangible. What takes courage is to become vulnerable, to take a chance, to
step into the unknown and ask to meet God yourself. What takes
free thinking is to ask for a relationship with the Creator. Whether
you're a believer or not, you've got to admit that takes guts. If it were
a science fiction movie, we'd all be on the edge of our seats wondering what would happen. The person who demanded proof would
have earned our scorn for having a closed mind.

Why have I let the blind define what sight is?

In real life, in our *enlightened* society, those daring risk takers are
seen as schmucks, when what they really are is curious, free-think-
ing truth seekers. Real revolutionaries.

· | · | · | · | · | ·

Think Outside the Box

Bobby: When I turn 18, I'm going to do whatever I want for the Lord. Tattoos, piercings, you name it.

Hank: Well, I'll take that chance. Come here, there's something I want you to see. (Hank takes down a box from the shelf and opens it up) Remember this?

Bobby: My beanbag buddy? Oh, man, I can't believe I collected those things. They're so lame.

Hank: You didn't think so five years ago. And how about your virtual pet? You used to carry this thing everywhere. Then you got tired of it, forgot to feed it, and it died.

Bobby (looks at a photo of himself in a Ninja Turtles costume): I look like such a dork.

Hank: I know how you feel. I never thought that *Members Only* jacket would go out of style, but it did. I know you think stuff you're doing now is cool, but in a few years you're going to think it's lame. And I don't want the Lord to end up in this box.

King of the Hill

Trends fade. Things change. Our interests bounce like rabbits from one fad to another.

One never changes, remains eternal, is worthy of our unceasing attempts to connect.

We can't box him in. We can only box ourselves in. Think bigger. Love bigger.

• | • | • | • | • | •

Everyone's Special?

Dash: You always say, "Do your best," but you don't really
mean it. Why can't I do the best that I can do?
Helen: Right now, honey, the world just wants us to fit in, and
to fit in, we gotta be like everyone else.
Dash: But Dad always said our powers were nothing to be
ashamed of, our powers made us special.
Helen: Everyone's special, Dash.
Dash: [muttering] Which is another way of saying no one is.

The Incredibles

I vividly remember my pride in our children's discernment when
they would come home from grade school awards ceremonies and
disgustedly toss aside their "attendance" awards.

"These are worthless. Everyone got one. And *attending* is what
we're supposed to do anyway."

Precisely. The school was mistakenly trying to instill self-esteem
by demonstrating that every single child was special, worthy of an
award. *Special* by definition means something that only a few can
achieve, as the kids were well aware. So much for self-esteem via
universal award.

Brad Bird's humorous yet pointed look at family life in *The
Incredibles* hit the nail on the head. He underscored what all good
parents know about both self-esteem and being special.

Love your children unconditionally for themselves, for the
unique beings that they are. Hold them to a high standard of behavior and achievement, however, before lavishing them with rewards.

Your children know the difference, and good self-esteem comes from this distinction.

Now that I think of it, that is exactly what God does with us.

Who better to imitate in our own families?

. | . | . | . | . | .

Playing God Is Harder Than You Think

Hammond sighed and sat down heavily. "Damn it all," he said, shaking his head. "It must surely not have escaped your notice that at heart what we are attempting here [at Jurassic Park] is an extremely simple idea. My colleagues and I determined, several years ago, that it was possible to clone the DNA of an extinct animal and to grow it.... Since it was so exciting, and since it was possible to do it, we decided to go forward...."

"Simple?" Malcolm said. Somehow he found the energy to sit up in the bed. "Simple? You're a bigger fool than I thought you were. And I thought you were a very substantial fool."...

..."I'll make it simple," said Malcolm. "A karate master does not kill people with his bare hands. He does not lose his temper and kill his wife. The person who kills is the person who has no discipline, no restraint, and who has purchased his power in the form of a Saturday night special. And that is the kind of power that science fosters, and permits. And that is why you think that to build a place like this is simple."

"It was simple," Hammond insisted.

"Then why did it go wrong?"

Michael Crichton, *Jurassic Park*

Michael Crichton was a scientist, and many of the books he wrote were not only page-turning thrillers but also cautionary tales. The essential moral was that it is dangerous to use borrowed knowledge, because one hasn't done the hard work to earn the discipline to wield it responsibly.

We've seen this story before. Frankenstein. Faust. Adam and Eve. Like Crichton, I'm not against science. I am against doing something just because we can.

. | . | . | . | . | .

May the Hokey Force Be With You

> **Han:** Hokey religions and ancient weapons are no match for a good blaster at your side, kid.
> **Luke:** You don't believe in the Force, do you?
> **Han:** Kid, I've flown from one side of this galaxy to the other. I've seen a lot of strange stuff, but I've never seen anything to make me believe there's one all-powerful Force controlling everything. There's no mystical energy field controls my destiny! It's all a lot of simple tricks and nonsense.
>
> *Star Wars*

Star Wars pulls together so many classic story elements of a hero finding his destiny while giving us a rip-roaring good adventure. It is perhaps inevitable that sidekick Han Solo draws attention from farm-boy-cum-warrior Luke Skywalker. He is the good-looking scoundrel whose cynicism hides a heart of gold.

He is not the hero, but I find his story more applicable to modern life than George Lucas probably intended. We are living in a time when anything that is not concrete must be proven scientifically or it is mocked, loudly and repeatedly.

What is interesting about Han Solo is that by the movie's end, without any proofs or miracles, his heart has been softened and changed. The powerful witness of Luke, Leia, and Obi Wan have shown him something intangible that is of more value than a good blaster at his side.

It is through personal witness that any of us changes, either for good or ill.

Sometimes I think about how astonishing it is that Jesus did not write anything down. No one was taking notes either. He entrusted the future of the faith simply to witness. That is a foreign concept to us.

Person-to-person. Face-to-face. It is how twelve men took what they saw in Jesus Christ and changed the world.

It is how we can change the world again.

· | · | · | · | · | ·

Heaven and Earth Aren't What You Think

> On the evening of that first day of the week, when the doors were locked, where the disciples were, for fear of the Jews, Jesus came and stood in their midst and said to them, "Peace be with you."
>
> John 20:19

I don't know about you, but if I lock a room, I expect the only people to be in that room are those who were in there before I locked it. But what happens is Jesus somehow comes into the room. Maybe he just appeared to them *bing!* He's resurrected, I suppose maybe he could do that. But the point is he's not stopped by physics.

And I really like another intriguing theory of how he got into the room. It's that he walked through the wall.

How?

Not because he's a spooky, spirit ghost but because he was more dense and more substantial than the wall itself. A little bit like when you and I might walk through a morning mist....

God is spirit and rather than being inferior to material existence he's actually far, far greater. We live in the material world. We get so bogged down with it but the claim of Christianity is really that this [material world] is nothing. These are like shadows compared to the kingdom of heaven and nothing can stop God, nothing is impossible with God because He transcends everything, transcends physics and metaphysics.

Peter Laws, *The Flicks That Church Forgot* podcast

Talk about flipping my view of reality upside down!

Until I heard this I never thought about the fact that heaven is more real, more solid, more substantial than life here on earth. It absolutely makes sense, and I truly love that image of Jesus stepping through the wall as if it were mist.

It's rather like Plato's cave, I suppose, where the people are all looking at the shadows on the wall, thinking that they see reality. When in actuality all they have to do is step outside the cave to see the real world.

We're in the cave. Jesus is in the real world.

I feel oh so lucky, so blessed, that he steps inside the cave to be with us.

· | · | · | · | · | ·

Listen. What Do You Hear?

Tears were streaming down her cheeks, but she was unaware of them.

Now she was even able to look at him, at this animated thing that was not her own Charles Wallace at all. She was able to look and love.

I love you. Charles Wallace, you are my darling and my dear and the light of my life and the treasure of my heart. I love you. I love you. I love you. ...

Then suddenly he was running, pelting, he was in her arms, he was shrieking with sobs. "Meg! Meg! Meg!"

"I love you, Charles!" she cried again, her sobs almost as loud as his, her tears mingling with his. "I love you! I love you! I love you!"

Madeleine L'Engle, *A Wrinkle in Time*

I haven't read that book in years, but one morning I was forcibly put in mind of the passage above. That day's Pray-As-You-Go podcast focused on a reading from the Gospel of John.

As I listened, the soothing voice said, "'He calls his own by name and leads them out.' Pause for a moment to hear Christ utter your name. Allow him to repeat it again and again. Notice how he says it...."

I thought about this as I stepped into the shower. I listened. I heard the same thing again and again... in a mixture of words and images that excluded all other thought.

What filled my mind were Meg's words: "I love you. Charles Wallace, you are my darling and my dear and the light of my life and the treasure of my heart. I love you. I love you. I love you." And Charles Wallace running into her arms.

I haven't read that book for years, but Christ knew the precise words that would speak to this little sheep's heart, make tears run down her face, help her reconnect, and send her running into his arms.

. | . | . | . | . | .

Let It Flow

> When they heard this, they were infuriated, and they ground their teeth at him. But he, filled with the Holy Spirit, looked up intently to heaven and saw the glory of God and Jesus standing at the right hand of God, and he said, "Behold, I see the heavens opened and the Son of Man standing at the right hand of God." But they cried out in a loud voice, covered their ears, and rushed upon him together. They threw him out of the city, and began to stone him.
>
> Acts of the Apostles 7:54–58

The Bible is loaded with stories about the average Joe living his life as best he can according to God's will.

St. Stephen is often held up as the first martyr, whose enthusiasm for truth bubbled over into miracles, testimony, and public witness that just could not be stopped.

I often think of him as a passionate teenage boy, like many of our daughters' friends. Their enthusiasm can't be contained. They are like arrows shot straight to the target.

What I rarely remember is that Stephen was a deacon, assigned to take care of the poor members of the Christian community. It was a humble job, but his love was so much a part of his being that it overflowed into everything he did.

You still meet people like this if you keep your eyes open. I am often surprised by how many Christians I run across in daily life. Question is, I suppose, are they surprised by me? Do I hold it in or let it flow?

·　　|　　·　　|　　·　　|　　·　　|　　·　　|　　·

Do Chimps Read Plato?

> **Otto:** Don't call me stupid.
> **Wanda:** Oh, right, to call you stupid would be an insult to stupid people. I've worn dresses with higher IQs. I've known sheep that could outwit you, but you think you're an intellectual, don't you, ape?
> **Otto:** Apes don't read philosophy.
> **Wanda:** Yes, they do, Otto, they just don't understand it.
> *A Fish Called Wanda*

Do we really know all that we think we do? A bit of searching on the Internet, a few good quotes, maybe even an article or two later, and too many of us feel qualified for philosophic debate.

This is not to say that we can't argue logically or discuss philosophy without a degree, but we need to be firmly grounded in the truth of what we believe. Further reading might be required, admitting we don't know, or even having to reexamine beliefs based on what we have learned.

It can hurt. Believe me, I know. I had to be slapped around by lots of reading and the logic of two thousand years of Church teachings before I came to my current views about the sanctity of life in every form, including the unborn and the death penalty. I could almost feel the "rip" in my chest when I had to change my mind on these, especially when it came to admitting them to others. Those aren't popular views.

Once I really understood, however, there was no going back. That's the price of understanding what we think.

. | . | . | . | . | .

Faith and Priorities

The problem with faith...is it kind of screws up your priorities. Your priorities shouldn't be about saving your own a**, which is the focus of Christianity.

Bill Maher

There would be no more pagans if we were true Christians.

St. John Chrysostom

It may surprise you to know that I feel a certain sympathy for Bill Maher, who obviously has not been privileged to run into a Christian truly living in a Christlike fashion. The Christians I knew about when growing up were nice enough people but nothing extraordinary. Just like us. Except that they spoke some kind of strange coded language, always were on TV wanting money, and had some very odd rules for living.

Bottom line: We don't know who is watching when we are going about everyday life. It doesn't need to be something big. It is the witness of lives lived faithfully and joyfully that stands out to others.

Which gives me food for thought. How faithful am I, no matter who is watching? What if someone just like Bill Maher is watching?

I know a couple of people who are more polite and less angry than he but who have just as little faith in Christians. Then too, more important than that is the fact that God sees it all anyway. What am I giving him to work with?

·　|　·　|　·　|　·　|　·　|　·

What If I'm a Sap?

> I suspect that a great many people would like to be merciful but are unsure of how to begin and afraid of being cheated. My advice is: take stock of your limited resources—time, money, mercy—and decide what to do with them. Then just try it! And if you're afraid of being cheated, cheer up. You've already been cheated by lots of other people besides the poor: the federal government, many prominent corporations, most financial institutions, and perhaps even some religious organizations!
>
> Fr. Benedict Groeschel

He really has a way of hitting the nail on the head, doesn't he? It is that fear of being a sap, a dupe, a simpleton that keeps us from being as generous as we should to those who very well may be in true need.

We can be wise about our charity while still being merciful. I never have cash on me but always have the car stocked with granola bars. Beggars I encounter are therefore offered food and also a little bottle of water in the summertime.

What I have been given, I have received through God's grace. I absolutely can look back and see how I have wasted it, thrown it away, wanted something else. In short, I myself have taken God for a sap.

How selfish and stingy of me if I do not give the same chance to others that he has offered to me time and again.

> Some will say, "Oh, he makes a bad use of it!" Let him make what use of it he will, the poor man will be judged by the use he has made of your alms, and you will be judged for the alms that you might have given and did not give.
>
> St. John Vianney

·　　|　　·　　|　　·　　|　　·　　|　　·　　|　　·

We Don't Like That Word

> Benedict paused as if contemplating the full extent of the scene he had described. "Nobody wanted war. All were acting in what they perceived to be their best interests. Yet their perceptions were so warped by their sins—you don't like that word, Chiang. Most of us don't. Perhaps I should date my conversion from the instant I realized that moral theology gave a more accurate account of human conduct than any school of psychology, because it understood that the basis of evil is intentional self-delusion."
>
> Robert R. Chase, *The Game of Fox and Lion*

My understanding of moral theology actually came after my conversion, when I discovered Catholic theology books. What amazed me was how logical it was, how beautifully all the pieces fell into place. I expected a soppy emotionalism. I found brilliant minds tracing the logic that follows from accepting that God exists and the wisdom of the Ten Commandments.

Human nature became much easier to understand.

I'm not talking only about sin and evil as Benedict does above. Love and sacrifice and redemption are pieces in a beautiful mosaic. They make up the perfection of the family unit as both a cornerstone of society and as our boot camp in the joys that accompany self-giving love.

It all fits in a way that embraces our most basic natures and that gives us a little window into the larger plan we inhabit.

When you have the key to human conduct, you have the key to everything. Including an open door to God.

. | . | . | . | . | .

Wrestling With Reality

> **Elwood P. Dowd:** Well, I've wrestled with reality for thirty-five years, Doctor, and I'm happy to state I finally won out over it.
>
> *Harvey*

Elwood's visions of his invisible friend, Harvey, bring great consternation to those around him who value sanity and reality according to their definitions. Indeed, most people would agree with their definitions, which would exclude a pooka who takes the form of a six-foot, three-and-one-half-inch-tall rabbit.

Haven't most of us had that same struggle at some time or other? Elwood is lucky enough to be able to see and hear Harvey. He knows that what most call "reality" is anything but. Of course, Elwood is fortunate enough to have the evidence of his senses. We don't have that luxury, unless we are one of those rare breed who are mystics.

We wrestle with reality ourselves and also with the world's definition of reality. On our side, solidly in this world with us, is the Church militant, the Church on earth. One of the many blessings of our Christian family is that we support each other in groping our way to the true reality, which cannot be measured or touched.

Invisible but surely true, reality is not the thing that most people think it is. It is worth wrestling with to have a true look at reality.

·　｜　·　｜　·　｜　·　｜　·　｜　·

God Doesn't Hand Out Cash

> **Damian:** I thought it was from God. Who else would have that kind of money?
> **Ronnie:** It's not really His thing, is it, handing out cash?
>
> *Millions*

Truer words were never spoken. However much we might wish to the contrary, God doesn't hand out cash.

God tends to use created things to answer prayers. Things, for example, like us.

Even as far back as Genesis, we see God creating the world and seeing "that it was good." He didn't whisk Adam and Eve into being from thin air but used earth and spirit, and also a rib. Jesus used mud and spit to heal the blind. There is copious evidence that, having made all that is around us, God expects us to use it.

That is what makes it all-important that we act on it and step up to do our part. Because using us to answer prayer, whether we may realize it or not at the time, is his thing.

. | . | . | . | . | . .

Can We Handle the Truth?

> Mr. A. always says it's not what you find out, it's what you do
> with what you find out. It's not people wanting truth, it's people
> not able to face it and lying instead. It's not even wanting to
> solve a problem for someone else, it's trying to find yourself.
>
> Liz Parker, *A Confidential Agent*

Exploring truth is one of those topics that mystery stories explore
again and again. Murder, blackmail, swindles, and extortion are all
presented to us in the interesting form of mental puzzles. Can we
solve the whodunits before the detective? Can we solve them at all?
Inevitably what is found in sifting through motives, clues, and sus-
pects are people who are not adjusted to reality, who can't face truth
and will do anything to maintain their dreams.

This isn't confined to mysteries, naturally. It forms a great part of
conflict in the world. Country versus country, group versus group,
even, sadly, friend versus friend. We are much more addicted to our
own views than to giving up that bit of our identities and trying to
truly find ourselves.

The definition of true humility is to see clearly where we fail and
where we succeed. Humility is asking for God's grace to make up for
our deficiencies and acknowledging his good in bestowing our tal-
ents. In true humility there is no mystery.

. | • | • | • | • | •

Making God in Our Image

God: Let me explain something to you, Joan. It goes like this: I
don't look like this. I don't look like anything you'd recognize.
You can't see me. I don't sound like this. I don't sound like anything you'd recognize. You see, I'm beyond your experience. I
take this form because you're comfortable with it. It makes sense
to you. And if I'm "snippy" it's because you understand snippy.
Do ya get it?
Joan: Sort of.
God: Good, 'cause I'm really not snippy. I've got a great per-
sonality. You'd like me.

Joan of Arcadia

That is a very interesting concept to consider. What does it mean
if our limitations shape how we see God? What sort of person
would appear before us if we were in Joan's shoes? Vengeful?
Sentimental? Persnickety?

One of the great things about the television show *Joan of Arcadia*
was that it clearly reflected the truth that we can't possibly know God
but that in our insufficiencies we can still see some facet of him and
perhaps advance a step closer.

We see those reflections all around us wherever the truth is told.
Quite a lot of TV, movies, books, and music have a heavenly reflection if we simply keep our eyes open. We must be alert enough to
sort the kernels of truth from the distortions of reality that our own
longing adds. We are entertained along the way. Nobody said we
can't have a good time while we're looking for truth.

Jesus attended a wedding, made enough wine to keep the party going in grand style for three days, and began his ministry. All in the same afternoon.

Now, how many do we suppose simply were delighted in the taste of the wine, and how many saw something more? That is our challenge.

· | · | · | · | · | ·

No Excuses Allowed

> Don't say, "That's the way I am—it's my character." It's your lack of character.
>
> St. Josemaría Escrivá

There are a lot of old practical proverbs that have been forgotten. So have the virtues they espoused. A penny saved is a penny earned. A stitch in time saves nine.

Have we forgotten them because they represent a hard way to live? It is easier to let things slide a little, relax, enjoy life, and not be so rigid all the time. These days we tend to be better at excuses than virtues.

I'm as much for enjoying life as the next guy, but every time I slide out of my good habits and try to claw my way back, St. Josemaría Escrivá's words come back to haunt me.

Is it that distractions are too powerful? Do I deserve to relax because I've worked hard? Or is it simply easier to think about doing something than to deny myself and simply begin?

I don't think this is a new problem. Not if we remember that Lao-tzu (604–531 BC) coined one of the most well-known sayings about the virtue of simply beginning: "A journey of a thousand miles begins with a single step."

Each day I have the chance to take that step and then another.
No more excuses. Let us begin.

· | · | · | · | · | ·

Will There Be Pizza in Heaven?

"Who cares," my interlocutor asked, "about butterflies in Brazil
or the chemistry of distant stars?" The short answer is that God
cares, because he bothered enough to make them.

Michael Baruzzini

It can be very tempting to focus on the lofty things and ignore the
simple, material things. Is it an American tendency to want to sort
everything neatly into little boxes and then just focus on the one that
interests us most? Perhaps it is simply how humans think.

I have rhapsodized elsewhere in this book about simple pleasures
and could go on longer about the delights of watching sparrows at
the feeder, of a cold glass of homemade lemonade on a hot day, or of
the scent of wild roses.

The truth is that we need both the lofty thoughts and the simple
pleasures. We're both spirit and body, just as was Jesus when he
came to live among us.

Jesus still had his body when he rose from the dead. If ever there
was a time for lofty thinking, you'd think it would have been after
being resurrected. Instead he showed the apostles the marks in his
hands and feet, ate fish with them, cooked them breakfast. If it's
good enough for Jesus, then it's good enough for me.

Are there butterflies in heaven? What simple pleasures might
await us when we are resurrected body and soul to live with God for-
ever?

· | · | · | · | · | ·

To Read or Not to Read? That Is the Question

If you don't read the newspaper you are uninformed; if you do read the newspaper you are misinformed.

Mark Twain

I'm a Mark Twain fan from way back. This sort of "damned if you do, damned if you don't" humor is part of the reason why.

It does leave us with a problem, doesn't it? Mark Twain is right, and we know it. So what does this mean?

We must be able to tell truth from fiction. We must not believe everything we are told. We must not jump to conclusions but must seek out truth from all angles, from more than one source.

If this is true for regular news, then how much more is it true about our faith? If we have questions about Catholic teachings, we need to go back and examine the logic that led to their current form. Make no mistake about it, there is reason and logic to those teachings.

I can hear you now, thinking, "Gee whiz. Can't she ever just laugh at something? Is it always about faith?"

It is my blessing and my curse, I suppose. While I'm laughing, I'm always thinking.

· | · | · | · | · | ·

Accepting Ourselves

There is one big thing we can do with God's help, that is, we can trust God's plan, we can put aside any quibbling or bitterness about ourselves and what we are.

We can accept and seize upon the fact that what we are at this moment, young or old, strong or weak, mild or passionate, beautiful or ugly, clever or stupid, is planned to be like that. Whatever we are gives form to the emptiness in us which can only be filled by God and which God is even now waiting to fill.

Caryll Houselander

It's OK to be fat. So you're fat. Just be fat and shut up about it.

Roseanne Barr

I was thinking about this when listening to A History of the World in 100 Objects podcast episode about the Olduvai stone-chopping tool. Someone used that stone tool 1.8 million years ago to chop bones, plants, and wood. Was that tool used by a person who fit in? Did he struggle with feeling bad about something that made him unacceptable to his group?

There have been countless standards of beauty, intelligence, and perfection over the ages. Just think of all the standards of conformity and correctness that have been imposed on people over the millions of years of human history. In many cases we look back and laugh at how arbitrary they were and how ridiculous the fashionable looked.

Why then do we not look at ourselves and realize that in many cases we are judging ourselves based on standards that are just as arbitrary? We can't see ourselves from far enough away to be dispassionate.

What if that very "defect" we despise is the door through which God is waiting to both fill us and enter the world for others?

• | • | • | • | • | •

Rowing Into Dark, Complicated Waters

... The old man spoke. "Do you like poetry?"

Assam thought of the school library, of Mrs. Jones desperately trying to steer the students toward more substantial and interesting ideas than adolescent wizard melodramas. Jane Austen for the cheerleader types, Jack London for the sports, Tolkien and Bradbury for the geeks and power dorks.

And then, for others, for students who seemed ready to abandon the mainstream completely for the uncharted backwaters of literature, she helped them find Poe and Lovecraft, Gaiman and Card and Ellison, Eliot and Parker.

Assam had rowed his canoe into those dark, complicated waters many, many times. So he answered, "Yes, I like poetry."

T.M. Camp, *Assam & Darjeeling*

This brilliant tale of two children seeking their mother weaves myth, literature, fairy tales, and original storytelling about love, sacrifice, and redemption. Best of all, it is a rattling good yarn.

It is not surprising that an author who adroitly combines so many literary allusions should pen such a spot-on assessment of whom these books would be likely to tempt into a larger world of reading. I myself have had to be lured into new reading, especially when it is a "classic" that has been plumped into some category or other. I had to be tempted into reading *Uncle Tom's Cabin* by my daughter reading excerpt after excerpt. It is now a favorite book that I push at others like a store offering free samples. It also began a new way of reading for me, as I hesitantly would select a classic and work my way through it.

If I had not pushed myself to read Dante's *Divine Comedy*, I would have missed many of Camp's references in his book. Gradually I am learning to be less wary and to see that those dark, complicated waters not only open a new world but enable us to better understand the world we already inhabit.

. | . | . | . | . | .

Make 'Em Laugh

Nothing shows a man's character more than what he laughs at.
                                        Johann Wolfgang von Goethe

True enough. I wonder what Goethe would have made of these fellows?

In the beginning there was nothing, which exploded.
                                        Terry Pratchett

In the beginning there was nothing, and God said, "Let there be light," and there was still nothing, but everybody could see it.
                                        Dave Thomas

Protons have mass? I didn't even know they were Catholic.
                                        Anonymous

I was thrown out of college for cheating on the metaphysics exam; I looked into the soul of the boy next to me.
                                        Woody Allen

When I told the people of Northern Ireland that I was an atheist, a woman in the audience stood up and said, "Yes, but is it the God of the Catholics or the God of the Protestants in whom you don't believe?"

Quentin Crisp

Now that I think of it, what would Goethe have made of me for laughing at them?

. | . | . | . | . | .

Spring in Without Fear

Facing his own death, a man turned to his doctor, as he was preparing to leave the examination room, and said, "Doctor, I am afraid to die. Tell me what lies on the other side."

Very quietly the doctor said, "I don't know."

The dying man said, "You don't know? You, a Christian man, do not know what is on the other side?"

As the doctor was holding the handle of the door, from the other side came a sound of scratching and a dog whining, and as he opened the door, a golden retriever sprang into the room and leaped on him with an eager show of gladness.

Turning to the patient, the doctor said, "Did you notice my dog? He's never been in this room before. He didn't know what was inside. He knew nothing except that his master was here, and when the door opened, he sprang in without fear.

"You see, I don't know what is on the other side of death, but I do know one thing. I know my Master is there, and that is enough."

Apocryphal

As I have gotten older, I realize that the moment of death is something real I will have to face—not just intellectually but in solid truth. Struggling with the reality of my helplessness, I came to one conclusion. The only thing that I will be able to do is to trust Jesus to get me through it.

When that time comes, will I know my loving Master is on the other side of the door? Will I gladly spring in without fear?

That is a hard idea to grasp at the moment. I think I have more work to do on really loving and trusting my Master.

· | · | · | · | · | ·

How Often Must We Turn the Other Cheek?

> Then Peter approaching asked him, "Lord, if my brother sins against me, how often must I forgive him? As many as seven times?"
>
> Jesus answered, "I say to you, not seven times but seventy-seven times."
>
> Matthew 18:21–22
>
> But I say to you, offer no resistance to one who is evil. When someone strikes you on [your] right cheek, turn the other one to him as well.
>
> Matthew 5:39

We're all used to the idea of having to forgive endlessly. The reality can be much more difficult and sometimes turn into an endless internal battle.

Thinking this over, I realized suddenly that not only must we forgive seventy times seven but we must be prepared to turn the other cheek that many times as well.

I don't know why it never occurred to me before how intimately linked those two teachings are. Someone may need continued forgiveness because there are repeated offenses for which they won't apologize.

Once is bad enough, but multiple times? That is a sobering thought, both for our capacity to take punches, so to speak, and to forgive them.

· | · | · | · | · | ·

Exactly Where You Ought to Be

> **Book:** I've been out of the abbey two days, I've beaten a lawman senseless, I've fallen in with criminals. I watched the captain shoot the man I swore to protect. And I'm not even sure if I think he was wrong.
> **Inara:** Shepherd. . .
> **Book:** I believe I just...I think I'm on the wrong ship.
> **Inara:** Maybe. Or maybe you're exactly where you ought to be.
>
> *Firefly*

When the battle is most hard-pressed is when heroes are called to help save the day. It may not feel like it at the time, but it is absolutely true.

We may not feel like heroes at the time, but that doesn't mean that we aren't acting heroic. It is a rare circumstance when the hero begins the battle at a set time under specific rules.

For most of us the battles come at odd times when we are in seemingly ordinary situations. Make no mistake, however, we are all called upon to be heroic.

Sometimes it is in the holding back of a sarcastic remark, sometimes it is in letting someone else take credit, and sometimes it is in
simply doing what we should. It is nothing that anyone would make
a movie about, and often we might feel that we are doing the worst
job ever in behaving as we should. That doesn't mean we aren't
heroes though. Or needed right where we are.

·　|　·　|　·　|　·　|　·　|　·

You Need Backup

Marcus: Suddenly I realized—two people isn't enough. You
need backup. If you're only two people, and someone drops off
the edge, then you're on your own. Two isn't a large enough
number. You need three at least.

About a Boy

We have all known the long loneliness and we have learned that
the only solution is love and that love comes with community.

Dorothy Day

If you want to see a vivid illustration of Dorothy Day's quote, watch
About a Boy. Will, a lead character, has a delightfully indulgent life
full of enjoyment. Being an "island" is not something he drifted
into. It is his specific goal.

On one level he is right because community can be, frankly, very
annoying. Certainly it means we don't get our own way as much as
we would like.

On the other hand, without community there are none of those
soaring moments of happiness, love, and celebration. As little as we
like to admit it, we might also need those annoying moments with

97

others to help smooth off our own rough edges and make the happiness possible at all.

One is not enough. Two? Nope. Three—a trinity, if you will—is needed.

At the very least.

· | · | · | · | · | ·

Reality Check

> In the world you will have trouble, but take courage, I have conquered the world.
>
> John 16:33

> And behold, I am with you always, until the end of the age.
>
> Matthew 28:20

Christianity isn't a religion of rainbows and lollipops. It is a religion that acknowledges the reality of human sufferings, hardships, and daily difficulties.

Like a lot of people, I tend to forget this when my life is whirring along pleasantly. Then, when things take a turn for the worse, I feel put upon. That's when I have to remember to do a reality check. I shouldn't be whining, "Why me, O Lord?" as if I have some ticket to an easy life. Reality is to acknowledge just the opposite. God doesn't change the world to make our lives easier, but he changes our focus to help us see what is happening below the surface.

Suffering doesn't mean we've gotten it wrong. God doesn't send it as a punishment. He came himself to help us through it, sometimes in spite of our own actions.

If we call on him for help, he is already there beside us. Not to hand over the obvious solution to a problem, although that does sometimes happen, but to support us and help us grow internally, despite sufferings.

What we think of as "reality" isn't everything. There is more. We just can't see it without God's grace.

· | · | · | · | · | ·

Calculating Halfway

Me: I remember reading this book [*Calculating God* by Robert R. Sawyer] a long time ago. I also really enjoyed it...until the end, which I felt was a real cop-out à la one of Gene Roddenberry's favorite scenarios.

Robert R. Sawyer: ...Oh, and Julie D, interesting blog you've got ("Happy Catholic: Not Always Happy, But Always Happy to Be Catholic"). We're obviously not going to see eye-to-eye [:)], but in my humble opinion, the only "real cop-out" would have been not to provide answers to the questions raised in the book.

They may not be the answers you'd have liked to see, but a cop-out, by definition, is ducking the questions asked (whether or not God exists, and, if he/she/it does, what his/her/its actual nature might be, and whether or not science can mean-ingfully address these points), and I most assuredly did not avoid answering those questions. :)

Robert R. Sawyer, commenting on the SFF audio review
of his book *Calculating God*

You run into people like this sometimes. They are so wedded to an idea that they repeatedly misrepresent an opponent's position. Then they knock it down to their satisfaction, the way that Sawyer did above when he made the conversation about religion instead of plotline.

Our society is full of these "halfway" men these days. They're not willing to risk a completely honest discussion and see where the truth leads them. They just want to defend their chosen position without ever brooking any opposition. That's always a huge disappointment to me. Whatever happened to the fine art of debate? Whatever happened to seeking the truth, no matter the cost? I suddenly feel as if I understand Diogenes' carrying a lamp in the daytime looking for an honest man in a way I never did before.

> I can accept anything, except what seems to be the easiest for most people: the halfway, the almost, the in-between.
>
> Ayn Rand, *The Fountainhead*

· | · | · | · | · | ·

Where's Your Messiah Now?

> "Be a man!" said I [to the curate]. "You are scared out of your wits! What good is religion if it collapses under calamity? Think of what earthquakes and floods, wars and volcanoes, have done before to men! Did you think God had exempted Weybridge? He is not an insurance agent."
>
> H.G. Wells, *The War of the Worlds*

Exemption from calamity is a criterion that nonbelievers often apply when judging Christians. They'll look at a disaster and joke about the terrible things that God's people must have done to feel his wrath. Or words to that effect.

They can be forgiven for using a false criterion because they don't understand that God is working with us internally, using outside circumstances as a catalyst to help us grow and mature.

What about us though? Christians can be just as bad about thinking that a faithful life means exemption from disaster. There is a great temptation to wonder where God is when tornadoes strike, tsunamis hit, or Martians land. We forget that he never promised us a rose garden. We live in the real world where tragedy can strike unexpectedly at any time.

As H.G. Wells so aptly put it, we are not insured against calamity. What we are promised is that God will always be with us, helping us bear the trials that come our way. God's insurance policy promises we will never be alone. That is a reality that can hold up no matter where we are.

· | · | · | · | · | ·

Seeing in a Whole New Way

"And do you know, Captain, that I have heard men sneer at—what do they call? A respectable man of full age—suddenly discovering what it is to love another person. Doubtless you yourself know what they say."

Sun Wolf had the grace to blush.

But if a man who has been crippled from childhood is healed at the age of forty will he not jump and dance and turn cartwheels like a young boy, scorning the dignity of his years? The mockers are those who themselves are still crippled. Think nothing of it."

Barbara Hambly, *The Ladies of Mandrigyn*

I was always one of those people who tended to think of deathbed conversions as less than sincere, rather like a drowning man clutching at a reed. It is rather hypocritical of me to think so, because I have to defend my own conversion fairly often against claims that I am clutching at a weak reed to help me make it through life.

Then my father died, and I saw a miraculous transformation take place. It was as if layers of rubbish that living had piled on were sloughed off. We could see the real man beneath. Those layers were a large part of what got in Dad's way in considering God and faith. Nothing focuses thought like the imminent death. With extraneous layers gone, he finally was able to consider it honestly.

When he talked to each of his six grandchildren on Skype and told them, "This is not the end. I am going to be waiting for you on the other side," it was not the action of a desperate and drowning man. It was with the clarity of someone who has seen the truth and chosen to believe it.

I now realize that, just as in my own conversion, or those who suddenly fall in love at an advanced age, those who convert on their deathbeds are doing so because they suddenly are struck by the truth in a completely new way.

> I once was lost but now am found,
> Was blind, but now I see.
>
> John Newton, "Amazing Grace"

· | · | · | · | · | ·

What Does "Happy" Mean?

> Miss Celia stares down into the pot like she's looking for her
> future. "Are you happy, Minny?"
>   "Why you ask me funny questions like that?"
>   "But are you?"
>   "Course I's happy. You happy too. Big house, big yard, hus-
> band looking after you." I frown at Miss Celia and I make sure
> she can see it. Because ain't that white people for you, wonder-
> ing if they are happy enough.
>
> Kathryn Stockett, The Help

Minny is the black household servant. Miss Celia is her employer. It
is 1962 in Jackson, Mississippi. We can see why there might be a
disconnect between what they think of as "happy."

Minny's comment makes me laugh because it is so true. How
many people fret themselves into despondency wondering if they
are happy enough when actually they are living lives that many
would envy?

On the other hand, readers know that both Minny and Celia have
problems that won't be settled by having a big house or big yard.
Sometimes there are problems that even a doting husband can't
help. Appearances are deceptive, as Minny learns. The question for
them, as for all of us, is whether our heart's desire is something that
matters or something that is a false dream of happiness.

· | · | · | · | · | ·

Who Does? Nobody

"Who did you pass on the road?" the King went on, holding out his hand to the Messenger for some hay.

"Nobody," said the Messenger.

"Quite right," said the King: "this young lady saw him too. So of course Nobody walks slower than you."

"I do my best," the Messenger said in a sullen tone. "I'm sure nobody walks much faster than I do!"

"He can't do that," said the King, "or else he'd have been here first."

Lewis Carroll, *Through the Looking Glass*
(And What Alice Found There)

Is there anything as delightful as the word play that Lewis Carroll used in his books? Perhaps it is only matched by that in *The Phantom Tollbooth* by Norton Juster. I am not sure that you could read either aloud to someone, as understanding the puns is so dependent on seeing the spellings and usages. Just imagine the explanations that would be required.

We think that we always understand what is being said, but do we? Are we using common references? common cultural understanding? common context?

Or do we simply jump to conclusions without stopping to listen well enough, to question, to know the context? E-mail and texting have led us into sloppy writing and speaking that depend on shorthand. I frequently hear that it is impossible to convey context in an e-mail. Not so. We are just too lazy to take the time to either write or read carefully enough to be sure we understand. Nobody does.

And if Nobody does, then we should be able to too.
Right?

. | . | . | . | . | .

Absolute Truth

> **Dr. Gregory House:** Right and wrong do exist. Just because you
> don't know what the right answer is—maybe there's even no
> way you could know what the right answer is—doesn't make
> your answer right or even OK. It's much simpler than that. It's just
> plain wrong.
>
> *House, M.D.*

Watching Dr. Gregory House, brilliantly acted by Hugh Laurie, is
somewhat like I imagine it must have been to know one of the more
irascible saints. In these "correct" days of moral relativity, it is
extraordinary for a television show to examine controversial subjects so consistently from every angle. Perhaps they get away with it
because House is not interested in making anyone like him. His
voice cuts like a sword through politics, emotions, desires, and all
the ways we interpret things to make ourselves more comfortable.
Those interpretations are what House would call lies. He'd be right.
This makes me think of the Sermon on the Mount. Jesus tells the
listeners a lot of contradictory-seeming statements beginning with,
"Blessed are the poor in spirit, for theirs is the kingdom of heaven"
(Matthew 5:3). I've seen the Beatitudes interpreted numerous ways
to allow us to live with them and not change much about our way of
life.

Truth is, however, a harder pill to swallow. Jesus was not deliver-
ing a sugarcoated intellectual statement. He was telling us the truth.

He was saying that the people of God can't be too comfortable in this world. There are rewards, but there is nothing comfortable about how we get there.

We are a pilgrim people. This is a way station, and heaven is our home. We can't afford to "go along" and lose clear vision of our true goal. It's just plain wrong.

· | · | · | · | · | ·

My Dog and Heaven Too

> The great pleasure of a dog is that you may make a fool of yourself with him and not only will he not scold you, but he will make a fool of himself too.
>
> Samuel Butler

> I can't think of anything that brings me closer to tears than when my old dog—completely exhausted after a hard day in the field—limps away from her nice spot in front of the fire and comes over to where I'm sitting and puts her head in my lap, a paw over my knee, and closes her eyes and goes back to sleep. I don't know what I've done to deserve that kind of friend.
>
> Gene Hill

What is it about dogs? There can be something sublime about the affection of man and dog, as we love a creature that is so different and yet understands us so very well. Perhaps they are our link to the natural world, as close as we can get to the way things should be, the way life is in heaven. If that is the case, then we have assurances here on earth that heaven will indeed be perfect.

· | · | · | · | · | ·

Playing Around Is Serious Work

> ...[N]o special sacrifices or rites are prescribed for the sabbath:
> the whole community, and even animals, render homage to
> God by ceasing from their labors.
>
> Commentary on Exodus 20:8–11, *The Navarre Bible*

> God rested, not because he was tired. God rested to cele-
> brate, to savor, to delight in, to play, to revel in the creation,
> to say, "It is good." God rested and declared it holy. In that
> rest, God is affirming that there is nothing to prove. We are
> invited to enter that rest. Sabbath is the invitation to rest from
> the tyranny of pursuit....
>
> Terry Hershey

I find it fascinating to think about the reminder from the Navarre
commentary above that God doesn't prescribe how we take rest. He
simply tells us to do so.

Rest, in and of itself, is holy.

This is a freeing concept, isn't it? It invites us to determine just
what rest is. This can be surprisingly difficult to do, as practitioners
of keeping the Sabbath will testify. Tom and I have been practicing
keeping the Sabbath for almost a year. We still struggle with not
doing things that can be marked off of a "to do" list. We continually
rediscover how addictive work is in our lives when we are struggling
not to turn on the computer or clean out that drawer or write up a
report. Conversely, we also rediscover how refreshing and just plain
fun it is to simply rest when we have successfully filled a day with
reading, games, or hobbies.

Make a serious effort to keep the Sabbath holy, even if only for an hour or two at first. It will make a difference.

·　　 |　　·　　 |　　·　　 |　　·　　 |　　·　　 |　　·

Pleasure Is Not Happiness

> The pity of it all is that people are so often frightened by the thought of the suffering that they may have to endure in the service and search of God, while in fact such sufferings are usually no greater than those which men often endure to ensure worldly success or the attainment of some cherished end—to say nothing of the fact that halfhearted service is the hardest service of all.... Our motto should be: Do manfully! And let it never be forgotten that pleasure is not happiness, nor is suffering sadness.
>
> M. Eugene Boylan, O.C.R.

This book was written over sixty years ago to help Catholics live their faith better every day. It was something of a surprise to me to see that, for the most part, the advice is as fresh as ever.

The advice about fearing suffering certainly hits home for me. In fact, I so often expect that I will shrink from doing something that I have made it a regular part of beginning my prayers: "Let it be done unto me according to your will, Lord. And I'm sorry that I'll probably be afraid of what you ask. Help me through it."

By now you'd think that I would know serving God has rewards beyond those I might be able to foresee. After all, God's will usually means doing what I should anyway: forgiving someone, speaking up about Church teachings, refusing to look for unfavorable motives in someone's behavior. You get the picture.

Sometimes I can keep that in mind. Sometimes, however, I can't. Those are the times that I make myself miserable by dodging, making excuses, and fighting with myself. Inevitably I feel like an idiot when I go ahead, do what I'm supposed to, and get some benefit I didn't expect.

I am as slow to learn as the disciples often were that God's ways are not my ways, his thoughts are not mine, and his plan is always better than mine.

. | . | . | . | . | .

Slogans Just Aren't Enough

> There's probably no God. Now stop worrying and enjoy your life.
>
> Atheist ad on London bus

> Sleep in on Sundays.
>
> Atheist ad on Chicago bus

More sleep. No worry. *Probably* no God? Interesting concepts but just a touch behind the times and illustrative of how Christians are often treated as stereotypes.

I don't know anyone who already doesn't sleep in late on Sunday if they want. The idea of being forced by guilt or society to go to church is an attitude that might have applied to churchgoers in the 1950s, but Americans, and presumably the English, have largely left that behind.

Anyone who can turn on a television set knows that worrying is not the prerogative of the faithful Christian. In fact, having gone from agnostic to Christian, I can tell you that a true believer has much less worry than someone who has no faith at all.

These bus signs actually are more of an acknowledgment of the lack of a true Christian example being set. People profess faith but don't examine their profession and all too often do not live it.

Above all, these ads are conversation starters for us, enabling us to talk about what we know and love about our faith. We can use them to express our joy and peace in having a person-to-person relationship with God.

If we can't have that discussion honestly, then the ads are a good jump start for self-examination of what we do believe, why we do not have the relationship we'd like, and what we might be missing by sleeping late on Sunday.

> Fight all error, but do it with good humor, patience, kindness, and love. Harshness will damage your own soul and spoil the best cause.
>
> St. John Cantius

· | · | · | · | · | ·

What Is Worthy of Belief?

> "I believe," he thought. "I have faith."
>
> He jaunted [teleported] again and failed again.
>
> "Faith in what?" he asked himself, adrift in limbo.
>
> "Faith in faith," he answered himself.
>
> "It isn't necessary to have something to believe in. It's only necessary to believe that somewhere there's something worthy of belief."
>
> Alfred Bester, The Stars My Destination

There is a thoroughly modern idea that it doesn't matter what you believe in as long as you believe in something. I have always found this rather disingenuous. We can believe in many things that are not good for us and follow them into the depths of despair when they don't prove to be trustworthy.

That is why I like Alfred Bester's approach. He tells us, essentially, that if we keep seeking we will find, if we knock long enough the door will be opened. If something is "worthy of belief" and we keep looking for it, then at some point we will find out what it is. Bester's argument falls apart at that point, since he may not know just what he believes in, but that sense of optimism is in itself worthy of belief.

Without having such a clear formulation, I suppose that was what I did as I continually came back to the question of God's existence. Until the question was answered as a definitive "no," then I was going to keep asking the question and looking for the truth. Of course, I found that the answer was instead "yes."

Which is another way of saying that Bester was right. There is something, someone, worthy of our belief. We must simply ask and then keep our eyes open. There will be an answer.

· | · | · | · | · | ·

Answering Life's Questions on the Silver Screen

> You know what your problem is, it's that you haven't seen enough movies—all of life's riddles are answered in the movies.
> Steve Martin

> Art does not reproduce what we see; rather it makes us see.
> Paul Klee

Is it that art makes us focus better on what we are seeing?

Or is it that, as scientific studies consistently find,* we are "wired" to understand stories?

We can instinctively tell when a story is forced or incomplete or just doesn't hang together right. Our natural affinity for stories seems to work as a lie detector that kicks in when we view art. Someone can tell us a bald-faced lie disguised with facts and figures and we swallow it whole. However, if we watch a love story where the girl is choosing the wrong guy, we know it instinctively. There is a pattern of how life should be that is mirrored in art. We know how to pick it out.

Depending on our knowledge of different arts, we see this reflected there also. Paintings and music use different languages but still are telling stories and opening up the truth for us.

We may not be able to solve all of life's riddles, but if we are giving ourselves regular doses of honest storytelling, in whatever form, then we're going to have a leg up on handling the riddles we come across in daily life.

---

* See Jeremy Hsu, "The Secrets of Storytelling: Why We Love a Good Yarn," *Scientific American Mind*, August 2008.

·　　|　　·　　|　　·　　|　　·　　|　　·　　|　　·

How to Know Thyself

> If you are humble nothing will touch you, neither praise nor disgrace, because you know what you are. If you are blamed you will not be discouraged. If they call you a saint you will not put yourself on a pedestal.
>
> Blessed Teresa of Calcutta (Mother Teresa)

There has rarely been a more practical statement about humility than Mother Teresa's. Being humble doesn't mean being a downtrodden doormat, as the popular depiction would have us believe. Nor is it humble to adopt false modesty about one's good traits. Truly humble people can acknowledge where they shine as well as where they fall short.

Humility is exceedingly difficult. We love ourselves too much to be able to do a very good job of it. We don't want to hurt our feelings, and we like to pat ourselves on the back.

How do we do it? It is a repetitive process. Just as exercise builds muscles, looking at ourselves honestly builds humility.

I have found that God answers prayers for humility promptly and plentifully. I ask to be shown where I am falling short, what I need to work on to get closer to him. The next few days are full of moments that try my patience, tempt me to step into the spotlight and embarrass myself, and much more. He answers. Never fear.

What remains after that is to use our self-knowledge to turn to God for his grace and help in gradually transforming ourselves into the people he has created us to be.

> **Irv:** Derice, a gold medal is a wonderful thing. But if you're not enough without one, you'll never be enough with one.
>
> *Cool Runnings*

· | · | · | · | · | ·

The Secret Code

> She'd been strangled with a rosary—not a run-of-the-mill rosary like you might get at a Catholic bookstore where Hail Marys are two for a quarter and indulgences are included on the back flap

of the May issue of Nuns and Roses magazine, but a fancy heir-
loom rosary with pearls, rubies, and a solid gold cross, a rosary
with attitude, the kind of rosary that said, "Get your Jehovah's
Witness butt off my front porch."

Mark Schweizer, Bulwer-Lytton Fiction Contest 2007

You've gotta love being part of a Church that has such universal
identification with her symbols. It allows for a cultural shorthand
and sometimes, as above, for a lot of fun.

It also makes the Catholic Church a big target sometimes. In the
movies Catholic symbolism is often the stand-in for all Christian
faith. On television the media deliver a twenty-second sound bite
about the Church, and everyone begins basing their opinions about
Catholics on it. In daily life people think our devotions are superstition instead of a focus for growing closer to Jesus.

Worst of all, sometimes those people are...us. Too many
Catholics believe what Hollywood and the media say without any
critical examination. We don't dig deep enough into what is really
true. We don't know our faith well enough to defend it, even to ourselves.

Our faith is not the place to begin looking on the surface and
accepting easy answers. If we don't know, we should ask. If we hear
something disturbing, we should investigate. Those aren't the only
reasons, of course. The more we know about our faith, the closer it
should bring us to God. That's the best reason of all.

· | · | · | · | · | ·

Too Much Information

> We are all here on earth to help others; what on earth the oth-
> ers are here for, I don't know.
>
> John Foster Hall

I have an innate urge to "fix" things. Many of us do. We also like to
apply this to other people's lives. Suggestions, plans, and tweaking
are offered to those who we feel just don't understand. Surely they
would have done it the way we clearly see is best otherwise. Wouldn't
they?

Another word for this is *meddling*.

I believe meddling is the American way. Our culture teaches us to
be helpful. That seems a grand idea until we are the ones receiving
the endless stream of helpful advice for everything from curing back
problems to getting the best mileage to best prayer techniques.

None of this actually is a problem as long as we don't let all the
extra information distract us from what works for us. I am just now
getting back to the basic way that works best for me, after casting
around for several years following other advice about prayer techniques.

I try to keep this in mind when I feel that inner urge coming on to
speak up when I haven't been asked. It is a tough urge to resist, and
I love to share, but I'm trying hard to keep from becoming part of
the problem when I think I'm offering a solution.

It is a lesson we all need—to let alone the things that do not
concern us. He has other ways for others to follow Him; all do

not go by the same path. It is for each of us to learn the path by which He requires us to follow Him, and to follow Him in that path.

St. Katharine Drexel

· | · | · | · | · | ·

Spoonful of Sugar—Real Love

Love, in the true sense, is not always a matter of giving way, being soft, and just acting nice. In that sense, a sugar-coated Jesus or a God who agrees to everything and is never anything but nice and friendly is no more than a caricature of real love. Because God loves us, because he wants us to grow into truth, he must necessarily make demands on us and must also correct us.

Pope Benedict XVI

That sounds familiar somehow.

Someone who will put himself to the extra trouble of holding us to a higher standard because he recognizes our true potential.

Parental. Like a true father. Who loves each of us as if we were his only child.

Thanks be to God for higher standards and a Father who loves me enough to demand I live up to them.

• | • | • | • | • | •

Those Two Little Words

Homer Simpson: I never apologize, Lisa. I'm sorry, but that's just the way I am.

The Simpsons

…Children's security does not come from believing that their parents are infallible. It comes from observing that they are reliable, loving and fair.

By maintaining the posture that you are right when you are wrong, you would not only be exposing yourself as unfair, but you would be teaching them to bluster through their errors, rather than to correct them.

Miss Manners

It might seem like a no-brainer to say that one should apologize when one is wrong.

Believe it or not, I have met more than one set of parents who were really surprised by the concept of apologizing to a little one. Does it matter how old you are versus the age of the person you have wronged? Not really, unless it is to be able to tailor the apology to be appropriate to their youth.

As Miss Manners points out, if you think your children don't recognize when you are wrong, then you are fooling yourself. Living a life that is true to our values is more important than seeming infallible and also an excellent practice of our Christian lives. If we can't admit to our own children that we've made a mistake, then we have more to worry about than we realize.

· | · | · | · | · | ·

Oh, a Horrid Julie!

"I dare say it is rather hard to be a rat," she mused. "Nobody likes you. People jump and run away and scream out, 'Oh, a horrid rat!' I shouldn't like people to scream and jump and say, 'Oh, a horrid Sara!' the moment they saw me. And set traps for me, and pretend they were dinner. It's so different to be a sparrow. But nobody asked this rat if he wanted to be a rat when he was made. Nobody said, 'Wouldn't you rather be a sparrow?'"

Frances Hodgson Burnett, *A Little Princess*

This comes to mind whenever I look outside my kitchen window at our bird feeders. As often as not, I see a dear little…rat.

I can hardly blame it for enjoying a free buffet, but I don't like it because the feeder is actually for the dear little birds. Rats spread disease, reduce bird populations, and do plenty of other harm that I'm sure you already know about.

Sara's meditation does make me pause and ask what value we assign to life based on "cuteness." I now no longer resent the squirrels from poaching on the birdseed. When the common grackles let loose their machine-gun style calls sounding like a rusty gate, I remember that it has a value to them that I can't appreciate. All these types of life are here filling a niche that is perfect for them.

I also sometimes think about the people I see who are not too cute. Homeless men on street corners, self-righteous politicos, obnoxious telemarketers. Some have more choices about their behavior than others. The choice that I have, however, is to look a little deeper below the surface in every instance. My choice is remembering that "cute" does not always equal more valuable.

• | • | • | • | • | •

How Quaint

What mattered now was finding the right men [to commit a murder], and this was the foolproof idea he'd mentioned to Vinicius. He thought he'd use Christians. They seemed a lot more dependable and honest than the gutter sweepings with whom he spent his time in the squalid wineshops.... Judging everything by his own character and experience, especially since he'd barely bothered to scratch the surface of the Christian teaching, he assumed he would find willing tools for murder among them. Cynical as he was, Chilon was startled by the paradox that their scrupulous honesty made them his best choice....

"I wonder what he's like, this Hercules with flour in his hair," he mused while peering at the moonlit sky and the full white moon shining on the river. "If he's smart and vicious he'll cost me some money. If he's stupid, virtuous and a Christian, I'll get him for nothing."

Henryk Sienkiewicz, *Quo Vadis*

It is impossible not to relish the paradox of Christian honesty making the best murderers in this novel set during Nero's Rome. Add Chilon's belief that Christians are suckers, and it just increases how humorously he misunderstands the Christian faith.

It doesn't take living long ago to be misunderstood. It is startling how quickly Christianity has faded as an underpinning of Western culture. Coffee with friends can quickly turn into a no-holds-barred philosophical battlefield, with the Christian as a minority of one. Worse yet, you might find yourself quite taken aback when a

friend tells you with utter good will that Catholicism "is so inoffen-
sive in North America today so as to be almost quaint."

Quaint: odd, obsolete, or old-fashioned. The faith that martyrs
still die for today is... quaint. Quaint does not seem worth
fighting for.

Either they are missing something or we are. Is it our fault? Are
there so few good examples to be seen among Catholics living our
faith? What example am I setting? The only answer I know is to do
my best to be more than quaint and then leave the rest to God.

· | · | · | · | · | ·

That Little Twist

> It's a recurring theme in my books that Satan's chief power is the
> power of the lie. Any lie will do for him. He's equally happy to
> tell a Satanist that Darkness will conquer, or to tell a Christian
> that music with a back beat will inevitably lead to demonic
> possession. The way out is always to repent and submit to Jesus'
> lordship.
>
> Lars Walker

> **David St. Hubbins:** It's such a fine line between stupid and
> clever. It's just that little twist.
>
> *This Is Spinal Tap*

Usually, deep down, we know what is true. It is an easy thing for
Satan to give truth just a little tweak. We swallow it not only because
it is more believable but because we want to believe it.

Once that tweak has been believed, then Satan gives another little
twist, and we go down the rabbit hole again.

What hurts is that we go willingly.

What hurts even more is how little it takes for us to believe that lie.

He doesn't care if it is a lie that affects us individually or as a society. Whatever works.

It is our job to keep our eyes open so that we may evaluate what is really true and dodge giving in to the lies.

There is only one way out, and that is, as Lars Walker points out, the way Jesus walked for us first.

·　|　·　|　·　|　·　|　·　|　·

Oh, Grandma, What Sharp Elbows You Have!

Ever walk away from Mass feeling like the Holy Spirit has taken on your grandmother's voice, elbowed your ribs hard, and whispered in a tone that could cut steel to sit up straight and pay attention?

David Morrison

Haven't we all?

It's a moment of revelation that is blinding.

If you haven't had this happen, then you are either a saint or very good at ignoring Grandma. In which case, listen up!

·　|　·　|　·　|　·　|　·　|　·

Unbreakable

To love at all is to be vulnerable. Love anything, and your heart will certainly be wrung and possibly broken. If you want to make sure of keeping it intact, you must give your heart to no

one, not even to an animal. Wrap it carefully round with hobbies and little luxuries; avoid all entanglements; lock it up safe in
the casket or coffin of your selfishness. But in that casket—safe,
dark, motionless, airless—it will change. It will not be broken; it
will become unbreakable, impenetrable, irredeemable.

C.S. Lewis

Every time I read this I want to cry out, "No! Don't!"

I'm not sure who I'm crying out to.

Perhaps it is to so many people I see today who think that having
children would bring more problems than blessings.

Perhaps it is to people who won't even get a new dog or cat because
that would desecrate the memory of their previous beloved pet.

Perhaps it is to the lonely people I know who have been hurt one
too many times and so have given up on love.

I've learned through experience that being vulnerable is a fright-
ening thing. It can hurt. But it is better than being made of stone.

· | · | · | · | · | ·

Caterpillars and Butterflies

The first thing I would say is that all that this entails is at least one
hundred times harder on the parents than the child. A birth
defect by God's grace does not rob childhood of its wonder,
nor is a child burdened by high expectations. Given a support-
ive, creative, and loving family, I know personally that I enjoyed
not a less-than-average life, but as I've told many, my life has not
been ordinary but extra-ordinary....

"What the caterpillar calls the end of the world, the master
calls a butterfly." ...What we judge to be "tragic—the most

dreaded thing that could happen," I expect we'll one day see the awesome reason for the beauty and uniqueness of our life and our family.

Judy Squier, born with no legs, in a letter to parents
of a baby born with no arms or legs

We cannot avoid suffering. Even when we withdraw into ourselves so there is less vulnerability, smaller and smaller things cause us pain.

We are not always good at judging what might cause others intolerable pain. What we can do is to trust God in those circumstances that we cannot judge. He sees beyond our limited vision and fear of today to the butterfly of tomorrow.

Look around. You can't tell who was conceived with wine and roses and who was conceived on a street corner.

Juda Myers, conceived in rape,
Juda Myers Freedom Ministries

· | · | · | · | · | ·

Don't Tell Me What to Do!

Do you ever wonder why God values obedience more than sacrifice? Because obedience is someone else's idea of what you should sacrifice?

David Manuel

I hate to be told what to do.

I'm not alone in that feeling. As I have mentioned before, Americans are trained in independent habits from the cradle. That leaves us singularly ill-prepared to be obedient, especially if we have not had all the whys and wherefores explained. There is nothing wrong with wanting to understand reasons for a teaching or demand, of course, but we like to be in control.

That's part of the point, of course. We like to be in control. We are supposed to let God run things.

Forgiving someone seventy times seven. Loving our enemy. Turning the other cheek.

No wonder obedience is valuable. It is a rare and difficult thing.

. | . | . | . | . | .

Magic or Manners?

> "Can a magician kill a man by magic?" Lord Wellington asked Strange. Strange frowned. He seemed to dislike the question. "I suppose a magician might," he admitted, "but a gentleman never could."
>
> Susanna Clarke, *Jonathan Strange & Mr. Norrell*

Susanna Clarke captures in a nutshell an ethical question that has plagued man since the beginning of philosophy. Just because we have the capability to do something, does that mean we should do it no matter the consequences?

It is a question that asks us to consider past versus present, ambition versus humanity, and ruthlessness versus nobility.

It is not a question just for the big decisions of life either. It can be applied to holding the elevator for someone versus hurrying on to your appointment, pushing in line ahead of someone versus letting a mother with many small children go ahead of you, or running a yellow light versus losing ten minutes at a very busy intersection.

I'd like to think that I always choose the noble way. I know better though.

Small decisions, but they all add up to the answer to a very big question.

· | · | · | · | · | ·

Mirror, Mirror

> I had this whole thing about the dangers of collecting, about moving too close to the things you love and what happens when you become obsessed, what happens when you let your passions define you. Seriously, it was all done, all written, all ready to go.
>
> And I looked up at the bookshelf with upwards of 50 different role playing games and assorted supplements on it. And then I looked at the hundreds of DVDs.
>
> And then I looked at the books. Oh God, the books.
>
> Maybe I should stop being hypocritical and talk about something else.
>
> Alasdair Stuart

I hate to admit how many moments of self-awareness I have had just after smugly sorting out what someone else's personal flaw is.

You'd think that I'd stop sorting out other people's flaws, but I'm a slow learner, it seems.

The only good part is that I've gotten better at looking in the mirror earlier in the process. Then I go to confession, of course, because God already knows my sins and flaws and finger-pointing. He was just waiting for me to look up and see my own reflection in the imperfection I was contemplating.

Ouch.

· | · | · | · | · | ·

Oh, the Humanity!

According to a literary anecdote, the author Nancy Mitford had asked Waugh how he could behave so abominably and yet still consider himself a practicing Catholic. "You have no idea," Waugh replied, "how much nastier I would be if I was not a Catholic. Without supernatural aid I would hardly be a human being."

The New Criterion Reader

For most of my life I have had a "glass is half empty" attitude. Always quick to see the negatives of any situation and, even less attractive, always quick to dwell on those negatives. In the last few years, though, my attitude has taken a definite turn into optimism and joy. It is nothing that I have done for myself. If that were the case, I'd have figured out how to be happier years ago. Like anyone else I get frustrated, overwhelmed, stressed-out. Yet under it all is my great joy and gratitude to God for bringing me so far.

I do what I can to improve myself, but I look back at my life and see that it was God who nudged slowly toward peacefulness and contentment.

I fail. Oh, how spectacularly I fail sometimes. Yet God always helps me pick myself up, dust myself off, and glide into joy again.

· | · | · | · | · | ·

Cold, Hard Evidence

> I did not invent those pairs of differential equations. I found them
> in the world, where God had hidden them.
>
> Bernhard Riemann, nineteenth-century mathematician

I have friends and acquaintances who are atheists. They would like tangible evidence that God exists. Something they can measure and weigh and touch and smell.

I understand.

I tell them that our experience with God is not likely to yield cold, hard evidence. He is a person, divine and not human to be sure, but still someone we must relate to somehow. Our relationships with other people rarely yield something that a scientist can record as proof.

I myself, not knowing this at the time, actually did an experiment designed to see if God existed. I was tired of wondering, so I made a bet with him. If God were there, then he could give me something that I really wanted and I would know he existed. If no payoff ever happened, then I would know there was no God.

Nothing happened for a year, during which I rarely thought about my bet. Then I gave in. I had a change of heart. I decided that I did not need evidence God existed. I would take him on faith.

Naturally, the very next day God began paying off. I had to take that first step. I had to have a change of heart so that I would be able to recognize God when he delivered the evidence, just like Bernhard Riemann being able to recognize God's elegant design in our world.

I tell my friends that they only need to ask God to show himself to them. He will answer. If they keep their eyes open.

I like to think of conversion as a moment of surrender when you stop fighting.

Eric Brown

• | • | • | • | • | •

Oprahism

> **Tracy:** So, what's your religion, Liz Lemon?
> **Liz:** Hmm, I pretty much just do whatever Oprah tells me to.
>
> *30 Rock*

I don't have anything against Oprah. She does her level best to give good advice, and we could do a lot worse than to hear her out.

I myself like to look to Miss Manners for advice on living in this modern world. I'm a great believer in etiquette being a cure for what ails us.

As long as we're clear that Oprah doesn't trump Jesus, then we're OK. Yes, he even trumps Miss Manners, though I am sure she would quickly defer. That is simply good etiquette, after all.

• | • | • | • | • | •

One Link at a Time

> It is a mistake to look too far ahead. The chain of destiny can only be grasped one link at a time.
>
> Winston Churchill

This is what Mother Teresa called "living in the present moment." There is always a bigger plan in our minds, the things we will do "someday."

Yet we forget to pay attention to the here and now. We have to be careful that we don't end up wishing our lives away.

Those single links are things that it is impossible to get back once the moment is passed: a daughter's hug, my husband's wink as we cross paths at work, a stolen half hour talking with a friend during a chance encounter.

The present moment is where we live. Let us use it to advantage as we forge ahead to meet our destiny.

· | · | · | · | · | ·

The Monster in the Closet

> **Lois:** For crying out loud, that's no monster, that's your conscience. Be thankful God gave you one. It's a gift. And you know what most people do with theirs? They keep 'em in the closet all year, and only bring it out when they think he's coming to visit. You're not like that. Good for you.
>
> *Malcolm in the Middle*

Tom loved watching *Malcolm in the Middle.* As one of five brothers, he said that this show gave a real feeling of what it was like to grow up in a houseful of boys.

I looked at the outrageous comedy and wondered what he meant. It took me a while to recognize that under the extreme attitudes and situations there was real life being shown. However casually it was reflected, there was always a sense of what mattered, like the point Lois makes about following your conscience.

Conscience is so well understood by everyone, religious or not, that for Malcolm to think of it as a monster throws us off balance and becomes funny. Following up by speaking of it on television as a gift from God is so unusual as to call for headlines. Yet this was done so casually that it went unnoticed at the time, even by us loyal viewers. It was so powerful, however, that it is still one of the scenes that comes to mind whenever I am trying to ignore my conscience piping up about something.

Sometimes casual and funny is the best way to make a point anyway. None of us want to be preached at. The subtle points we understand later are sometimes the ones we remember most.

· | · | · | · | · | ·

If Jesus Grew Up in Minneapolis

> Nobody seems more obsessed by diet than our anti-materialistic, other-worldly, New Age spiritual types. But if the materialistic world is merely illusion, an honest guru should be as content with Budweiser and bratwurst as with raw carrot juice, tofu and seaweed slime.
>
> Edward Abbey

You don't have to be a New-Age type to practice this sort of reverse self-importance. My particular exposure has come through reading Catholic blogs where seemingly endless debates rage over things like wearing scapulars, whether Jesus went to school, and where that comma goes in what St. Thomas Aquinas wrote.

The end result? It makes me appreciate my husband for being the most basic kind of Catholic.

He loves the Church because of the truth, though he says that most people would not call his trust in the Church "love." He follows the rules because they are there for his good. He doesn't say novenas, say the rosary, wear a scapular, or do any other overt signs of

devotion. He simply lives his faith better than any other person I
have ever known.

More than that, he doesn't talk, talk, talk about it. Hardly ever. He
just lives it.

That is rare these days, no matter what your cause.

I mention this to him. He looks at me and says, "Isn't that what we
are supposed to do?"

Yes. We are here to be the salt of the earth, or if Jesus had grown
up in Minneapolis, the beer and brats of the earth. Let's get to it.

. | . | . | . | . | .

Basic Living Skills

"You've got to learn to do this yourself," I say, unscrewing the
Hellmann's button jar. "Okay, now, make the knot."

They make the knot. They stare at the knot. Then they wail, "I
can't do it! Can't you do it for me just this once, Ma? How can
you see what's under?" "I'm late, Ma." Or just, "Ouch!"

Sewing on a button, like avoiding eye contact on the subway,
is a basic life skill. Along with How to Windex a Mirror and
How to Make English Muffin Pizza, sewing on a button was
taught in the seventh grade by Miss Almeida in home ec. But
home ec isn't on the New York school curricula anymore.

Patricia Volk

I remember home economics. Half the year we learned cooking.
The other half we studied sewing. I am sure that somewhere in
between those large subjects were slipped lessons about hygiene,
cleaning, and other necessary life skills.

Home ec in school seems to have gone the way of drivers' ed, woodshop, and many other useful classes. That's too bad because simple exposure to many of these skills was all you needed to grasp the idea that, if need be, you were good at something besides writing an English paper or doing a science experiment. Now I find myself showing young adults how to make salad dressing. They are regularly astounded that one tablespoon of vinegar, four table-spoons of olive oil, and a little pepper form the basis for many of the world's great dressings (yes, including Caesar salad dressing).

There is a sense of accomplishment, of self-esteem if you will, that comes from not being dependent on others for your salad dressing or for sewing on a button. By removing these from high school, we are removing more than a simple domestic skill from our children's lives. We remove a richness and depth that is just as hard to replace as a button.

· | · | · | · | · | ·

Growth Through Adversity

> Is the Lord going to use you in a great way? Quite probably. Is he going to prepare you as you expect? Probably not. And if you're not careful, you will look at the trials, the tests, the sudden interruptions, the disappointments, the sadness, the lost jobs, the failed opportunities, the broken moments, and you will think, He's through with me, He's finished with me, when in fact He is equipping you.
>
> Charles Swindoll

I continually have to remember that growth comes from moments that I often don't enjoy.

The question I must continually remember to ask myself is, "Am I looking for the greater good in the middle of all this bad stuff?"

Am I asking God to show me where he is bringing good from moments where I can see no redemption at all?

· | · | · | · | · | ·

The Good News About Our Children

We didn't create our children, nor do we own them. This is good news. We don't need to blame ourselves for all their problems nor should we claim for ourselves their successes.

... They do not belong to us. They belong to God, and one of the greatest acts of trust in God is letting our children make their own choices and find their way.

Henri Nouwen

God doesn't have any grandchildren.

Anonymous

I cannot tell you how freeing it was when I read and absorbed these messages. I was a fairly new Christian, and my children were young. Like many young mothers I worried incessantly about my children's futures, the trials they would face, and the troubles they might encounter.

Somehow, though, the comment that God doesn't have any grandchildren made me suddenly focus on the reality that God deals with each one of us heart-to-heart. He has taken care of me this far, and he loves each of my children just as uniquely and just as much. He will not leave them either. It isn't on me.

Henri Nouwen then brought home the fact that we must help pre-pare our children to live, but we cannot protect them from life. We must trust them and trust God.

As I say, it is very freeing. For me and for my children.

· | · | · | · | · | ·

Perspective, Please!

Cardinal Cushing had an interview with a young priest who said to him, "Your Eminence, I am losing my faith."

The Cardinal said to him, "Meaning no disrespect to your intellectual attainments, but you and I are too dumb to lose our faith. The great heretics like Martin Luther lose their faith. You and I just get bored!"

Apocryphal

More than once, I've run into someone who has replied, "They made fun of Jeremiah, too," when he was ridiculed for saying something ridiculous.

Yes, and Alan Greenspan and I both chew our food before swallowing, but don't ask me to run a national economy.

Jeremiah is hardly the only figure in the Church whose mantle people like to assume on utterly trivial grounds. Are you obnox-ious? You must be as learned as St. Jerome. Do you complain about bishops? Gosh, when I close my eyes I can't tell whether you or St. Catherine of Siena is speaking.

Jeremiah wasn't a prophet because he was ridiculed. He was ridiculed because he was a prophet....

John da Fiesole

I always enjoy those little reminders that we're not as important as
we think we are. All it takes is thinking about Jeremiah, who wound
up stuffed headfirst down a well for his troubles. Then I am back to
knowing my rightful place at the bottom of the ladder... and being
darned grateful for it.

· | · | · | · | · | ·

The Measure of a Woman

> Strength is the capacity to break a chocolate bar into four pieces
> with your bare hands—and then eat just one of the pieces.
>
> Judith Viorst

Such a simple act.

Why is something so simple so awe-inspiring?

Is it because we rarely discipline ourselves enough these days to
not snack right before dinner, much less deny ourselves a square of
chocolate?

When did this happen to us? And how do we regain it?

I suppose the answer is right in front of us.

We do it one square at a time.

· | · | · | · | · | ·

Are You Ugly? I Can't Tell

> A person who has good thoughts cannot ever be ugly. You can
> have a wonky nose and a crooked mouth and a double chin
> and stick-out teeth, but if you have good thoughts they will shine
> out of your face like sunbeams and you will always look lovely.
>
> Roald Dahl, The Twits

Once you know someone well, it becomes more and more difficult to even remember if they are good-looking. It takes a long absence or dressing up for a special occasion to properly see them anew, the way everyone else does. We all know this, of course, but with the emphasis that is put on personal appearance these days, it can be easy to forget.

I try to remember that when I come across someone who has a stone face or who looks sour. Perhaps they are shy and are "hiding behind" their face. We can't all be lovely, and we can't all wear our hearts on our sleeve giving hints about what we're like. But we can give the chance for them to let the good thoughts shine out like sunbeams, lighting our hearts.

· | · | · | · | · | ·

The Long Defeat

> I am a Christian, and indeed a Roman Catholic, so that I do not expect "history" to be anything but a long defeat—though it contains (and in a legend may contain more clearly and movingly) some samples or glimpses of final victory.
>
> J.R.R. Tolkien

Anyone who has read *The Lord of the Rings* knows that a major theme is that evil is never completely vanquished and eventually rises again. No victory is ever final because in the future we will have to fight again.

This reflects Tolkien's completely Catholic view of our world, as did his books. It is a realistic viewpoint too, if we look at the long history of mankind with war after war. Our Bible tells us that Satan is the prince of this world (see John 12:31). Jesus' victory in procuring our salvation means that we will see triumph in the next world, but this world is more problematic. If Satan is running the place, then we know we've got our hands full because he wants our downfall. Period.

We must take the battle seriously because the outcome affects souls. We must always keep in mind that heaven is our true home. Our struggle is worthy and may, indeed, as Tolkien says, show us glimpses of final victory.

On a more cheerful note, we can remember that this same author gave us one of literary fiction's most endearing races, the hobbits. These little, comfortable folk love meals and parties and friends. They are chosen to undertake the largest of tasks, destroying the ring of power, and they show much resilience and bravery in their assignment. There is a clear message for us here too. No one is too small to make a big difference in fighting for victory.

. | . | . | . | . | .

A Generous Wife

A wife, if she is very generous, may allow that her husband lives up to perhaps eighty percent of her expectations. There is always the other twenty percent that she would like to change, and she may chip away at it for the whole of their married life without reducing it by very much. She may, on the other hand, simply decide to enjoy the eighty percent, and both of them will be very happy. It's a down-to-earth illustration of a principle: Accept, positively and actively, what is given. Let thanksgiving be the habit of your life.

Lars Gren

Simply put, don't try to change people. You can try to change yourself. You might even have some influence on the change in others because you have changed yourself. But don't fool yourself. You can't change someone else unless that person wants to change. As anyone who works in mental health will tell you, that is a rare occasion.

Take a good look at the person you will be spending the rest of your life with. Then look at yourself. Each of you will be enjoying 80 percent of the other. Ignoring that other 20 percent is not that hard when you realize that there are fully 20 percent of you that the other person is trying to ignore in turn.

How many psychiatrists does it take to change a light bulb?

Only one—but the light bulb has to *want* to change.

· | · | · | · | · | ·

Now I Have Found Happiness

> I looked for happiness everywhere: in the elegant life of the salons, in the deafening noise of balls and parties, in accumulating money, in the excitement of gambling, in artistic glory, in friendship with famous people, in the pleasures of the senses. Now I have found happiness, I have an overflowing heart and I want to share it with you.... You say, "But I don't believe in Jesus Christ." I say to you, "Neither did I and that is why I was unhappy."
>
> Hermann Cohen

Hermann Cohen was a brilliant musical prodigy in the nineteenth century, the favorite student of Franz Liszt, and an advocate of revolutionary ideas such as abolishing marriage and the right to unrestrained pleasure.

With that background, how did he come to write the letter we read a little of above?

Asked to substitute as choral director for a service in the Sainte-Valère Church in Paris, Cohen willingly did so and experienced "an indescribable agitation. I was, in spite of my own will, led to bend towards the ground." This experience began his conversion, after which he turned away from the world and became a Carmelite monk.

Hermann Cohen's life is a powerful witness to the change that we experience when we follow Jesus Christ. We cannot exude happiness all the time. It is impossible to ignore the evils and sorrows that daily life can bring. However, there is an internal gratitude and joy that we experience despite external circumstances. It is a happiness that sustains me through the bad and good, the happiness that is Christ in my life. How can we not want to share that with others, just as Cohen did?

· | · | · | · | · | ·

Here, There, and Everywhere

> And because I am a woman involved in practical cares, I cannot give the first half of the day to these things, but must meditate when I can, early in the morning and on the fly during the day. Not in the privacy of a study—but here, there, and everywhere—at the kitchen table, on the train, on the ferry, on my way to and from appointments and even while making supper or putting Teresa to bed.
>
> Dorothy Day

We like to think that we have less time these days than ever before. That isn't really true, as we can see from Dorothy Day's comments. Just as she did, we struggle to find time for prayer. These days we do have something she didn't, which is the opportunity for constant distractions from the Internet, iPods, and cell phones.

We must make a conscious decision to turn them off, to give ourselves some silence. It is only then that we can use all the little moments here, there, and everywhere to commune with God.

· | · | · | · | · | ·

My Big Fat Catholic Family

First, the good news about the Catholic Church is: It's like a big family.

Second, the bad news about the Catholic Church is: It's like a big family.

Mark Shea

Could he have said it any better?

We all know just what he means. We've all got family we love, family we wish we knew better, and family we can barely tolerate. Father and mother, sisters and brothers, the crazy aunt in the attic, the grandfather who always pinches your cheek too hard, the geeky second cousin who never wants to leave the house, and your aunt's second husband in the checkered suit.

Life is designed so that we're in it together with all our eccentric, eclectic relatives to learn about love and sacrifice and personal growth. That's what family is all about, right? Even if it begins with learning to be patient with that crazy aunt who bops you on the head with her handbag because you called your Catholic family fat.

. | . | . | . | . | .

The Most Moral Violence You'll Ever See

Ken: You didn't mean to kill a little boy.

Ray: I know I didn't mean to…. But because of the choices I made, and the course that I put into action, that little boy isn't here anymore, and he'll never be here again. [Pause]

Ray: I mean here in the world, not here in Belgium. Well, he'll never be here in Belgium either, will he? I mean, he might've wanted to come here when he got older. Don't know why. And that's all because of me. He's dead because of me. And I'm trying to… been trying to get me head around it, but I can't. I will have always have killed that little boy. That ain't ever going away. Ever. Unless… maybe I go away.

Ken: Don't even think like that.

In Bruges

This movie, about two hit men spending time in Bruges waiting for instructions from their boss, is one of the most violent and profane movies you could ever watch.

You wouldn't expect it to also be a thoughtful, interesting story about the powerful effect of extreme violence on the human beings who commit it. Above all, there are strong themes of second chances, sacrifice, redemption, and the potential to grow through suffering. In fact, it is the sort of movie that has a thoroughly Christian worldview, albeit one surrounded by flying bullets and constant swearing.

Hieronymus Bosch's painting *The Last Judgment* is a running theme throughout the movie, and gradually the movie becomes almost a mirror of the painting. A thirteenth-century painter about whom little is known today, Bosch incorporated in his paintings surreal and fantastic elements that are hard to understand unless one interprets them in the light of the religion of his day. While we may think we have a grasp on *The Last Judgment*, there are also surreal elements that are hard to integrate into the whole.

The creators of the movie intentionally mirrored Bosch's surrealism, but my guess is that they did not intend to show us a story mirroring Christian morality so thoroughly. We are simply fortunate that they cared enough about truth to follow the story honestly in examining the contrasts of violence and consequences.

We must look for truth just as unflinchingly, even when it shows us something that we do not think fits into how the world works. If we stay true to our goal, then we also will have a view of truth that works no matter what the circumstances. That should be every Christian's goal. Actually, it should be every person's goal. No one is less Christian than those hit men, but they show us truth nonetheless.

We have that truth available in everyday life, should we care to seek it.

Although, I hope, without flying bullets and constant swearing.

· | · | · | · | · | ·

Dante Lite

"Fortune tellers," Benito said before I could ask. "They tried to see the future by magic."...

Then I recognized one of the damned....

"Mrs. Herrnstein! Why?" I shouted....

"I was a good teacher with good pupils. But I could not be

bothered with the ones who weren't so bright. If they had trouble learning to read, I said they had dyslexia."*

"Are you here because of bad diagnoses?" This was monstrous!

"Dyslexia is not a diagnosis, Mr. Carpentier. It is a prediction. It is a prediction that says that this child can never learn to read. And with that prediction on his record—why, strangely enough, none of them ever do. Unless they happen on a teacher who doesn't believe in educationese witchcraft."

"But—"

"It was witchcraft, Mr. Carpentier. Please go now." She walked on, crying uncontrollably, her face toward us as she walked away. I watched until she was out of sight.

Larry Niven and Jerry Pournelle, *Inferno*

Dante is one of those guides who were geniuses at revealing the invisible world. Or so I was told. Frankly, I was never interested in reading Dante's *Inferno*. Those old classics are all good and well, but I don't need them. I can get those lessons in other places.

That was my attitude until one of my favorite pairs of science fiction writers found *Inferno* so interesting that they turned it into a modern book. Through their adaptation I discovered that you can see Dante's vision peering through the lens they used for adapting Catholic theology to specific, modern traits.

It is a wonderful book but also a sobering read. Dante reached over the centuries and through genre fiction to make me consider my own life in a light I hadn't before. I recognized that sins I thought were small and insignificant are actually no such thing. Niven and Pournelle weren't completely faithful to the original, as they rewrote some of the theology to please themselves. By the time I got to that part of the book, rewritten theology didn't matter, because I was so inspired that I went on to read the original and gain further insights.

I used to think that comic books and adaptations of classic works weren't worth wasting time on. I now know better. If a work is truly classic, then it has something to say to all of us, no matter how much later we may come along. If it takes a comic book to get me started, then so be it. A lite version may be just what I need to shed light in my life.

---

* Please note that the authors were pointing out that this teacher deliberately used the "dyslexic" label for any child she had trouble teaching to read, without actually bothering to find out if the child had any learning disabilities.

· | · | · | · | · | ·

Practice Makes Perfect

I despise recipes that promise results without work, or success without technique. I have eaten too many short-cut piecrusts to trust anyone who tells women that pastry made with oil is just as good as the "hard" kind. Mere facility, of course, is no more a guarantee of good taste in cooking than it is in music; but without it, nothing good is possible at all. Technique must be acquired, and with technique, a love of the very processes of cooking. No artist can work simply for results; he must also like the work of getting them....

Robert Farrar Capon

We hurry, we rush, we skip steps. All because we are told that this shortcut is "just as good" as the "old-fashioned" way.

Instead what we have found is that "just as good" isn't really all that great. The shortcuts haven't saved us any time, although they certainly have lowered the quality of what we consume. Personally I blame cake mix and canned frosting for drastically lowering the standard of American living. There just isn't any real substitute for learning by doing.

This is the point that Malcolm Gladwell makes in his book *Outliers*, where he claims that the key to success in any field is largely due to practicing a specific task for a total of around ten thousand hours.

I am not sure if this is true. However, I am sure that its origin is that old saying, "Practice makes perfect."

How do we do this in these busy, rushed, hurried days? We learn to say no. No to extra activities. We choose what is important to us and we practice it.

If our family is very lucky, what we want to practice is making cookies.

. | . | . | . | . | .

Bring Hope Out Into the Light

You know very well that a friendly voice is enough to set restless and troubled minds at ease. Be one of those who notice when the thermometer is rising, and not one of those who are always pointing out that it's getting colder.

...No, you are going to be the little smile which, though delicate, on certain winter afternoons reminds people of the springtime, and is its foreshadowing, and shows that the life and the joys of living are things that are still possible and not dead and buried.

> There are enough people who bury every budding hope.
> You, you be one who brings hope out into the light.
>
> Mother Marie des Douleurs

A lot of people show a marked tendency to gloominess these days, especially after the September 11 attacks. There is no need to be relentlessly or unrealistically cheerful like Pollyanna, but she did have one thing right. Looking on the bright side and gently encouraging others is a habit that can be cultivated. It is amazing the difference it makes, beginning with ourselves and going on to those around us. You really can help to bring hope into the light.

· | · | · | · | · | ·

The Church of [insert your name here]

Whenever I hear people talking about the need for Church reform, the first thing I ask is how they feel about obedience. Francis of Assisi was a strong, shrewd man and he was nobody's fool—but both he and St. Clare insisted on being obedient to the Church because Jesus was obedient to His Father, and they understood that our salvation comes through that submission of obedience....

And yet most of us treat the Church the same way we treat our flesh-and-blood mothers. We want the mother part, but we don't want the teacher part. We want her around to feed us, encourage us, and comfort us when things are going badly. But we don't want her advice, especially when it interferes with our comfort.

Archbishop Charles Chaput

I often think that Martin Luther would have been a great saint if only he had been able to separate the men in the Church from the Church itself.

He had so many good qualities. Just like Saint Francis.

He was charismatic and dynamic, and he wanted to grow closer to God. He was willing to suffer and sacrifice in order to do God's will.

Just two things were lacking. Trust and obedience.

He was not willing to be obedient to the Church. He was not willing to trust that God would speak to men and set things straight without Martin Luther's personal interference. Which was not like Saint Francis at all.

Saint Francis was also faced with a Church that wasn't in line with what God wanted. Yet while he strove to do what God wanted, Francis also obeyed the pope and trusted God to move things as necessary.

The result?

St. Francis founded a religious order, and the Church changed because of his example. Martin Luther began a series of protests that led to extreme violence and a church named after himself. Today we have countless little churches all believing different things.

I do not say this to be controversial. Some of the very best Christians I know, much better Christians than I, are Protestant. I wonder if we would have more saints among us, though, if these wonderful Protestants had the fullness of truth at their fingertips.

This isn't confined to Protestants, by the way. Within the Catholic Church there are many factions. The radical traditionalists nitpick about things like the lack of Latin in the Mass. Progressives pick and choose what teachings they will accept, just as the Protestants do. Both lack obedience, either by ignoring what is allowed or ignoring what is required.

We all would prefer to be in the Church of [insert your name here], it seems. It would certainly be more comfortable, although it may not be the path to heaven. We would do well to worry more about obedience and less about getting our own way.

> Martin Luther criticized Erasmus of Rotterdam for remaining in the Catholic Church despite its corruption, but Erasmus answered him: "I put up with this Church, in the hope that one day it will become better, just as it is constrained to put up with me in the hope that one day I will become better."
>
> Fr. Raniero Cantalamessa, O.F.M. CAP.

·　|　·　|　·　|　·　|　·　|　·

Christ With Me, Christ Before Me, Christ Behind Me
In the end, of course, Jesus is not just in our rearview mirrors. He is everywhere we turn our heads and hearts. We must just keep our hearts open so we don't pass him by.

St. Patrick's Breastplate
I arise today
Through a mighty strength, the invocation of the Trinity,
Through the belief in the threeness,
Through confession of the oneness
Of the Creator of Creation.
I arise today
Through the strength of Christ's birth with his baptism,
Through the strength of his crucifixion with his burial,
Through the strength of his resurrection with his ascension,
Through the strength of his descent for the judgment of
　Doom.
I arise today

Through the strength of the love of Cherubim,
In obedience of angels,
In the service of archangels,
In hope of resurrection to meet with reward,
In prayers of patriarchs,
In predictions of prophets,
In preaching of apostles,
In faith of confessors,
In innocence of holy virgins,
In deeds of righteous men.
I arise today
Through the strength of heaven:
Light of sun,
Radiance of moon,
Splendor of fire,
Speed of lightning,
Swiftness of wind,
Depth of sea,
Stability of earth,
Firmness of rock.
I arise today
Through God's strength to pilot me:
God's might to uphold me,
God's wisdom to guide me,
God's eye to look before me,
God's ear to hear me,
God's word to speak for me,
God's hand to guard me,
God's way to lie before me,
God's shield to protect me,
God's host to save me
From snares of devils,

From temptations of vices,

From everyone who shall wish me ill,

Afar and anear,

Alone and in multitude.

I summon today all these powers between me and those evils,

Against every cruel merciless power that may oppose my body
and soul,

Against incantations of false prophets,

Against black laws of pagandom,

Against false laws of heretics,

Against craft of idolatry,

Against spells of witches and smiths and wizards,

Against every knowledge that corrupts man's body and soul.

Christ to shield me today

Against poison, against burning,

Against drowning, against wounding,

So that there may come to me abundance of reward.

Christ with me, Christ before me, Christ behind me,

Christ in me, Christ beneath me, Christ above me,

Christ on my right, Christ on my left,

Christ when I lie down, Christ when I sit down, Christ when I
arise,

Christ in the heart of every man who thinks of me,

Christ in the mouth of everyone who speaks of me,

Christ in every eye that sees me,

Christ in every ear that hears me.

I arise today

Through a mighty strength, the invocation of the Trinity,

Through belief in the threeness,

Through confession of the oneness,

Of the Creator of Creation.

Amen.

SOURCES

pg. ix.   New convert, Catholic and Enjoying It blog, http://markshea.
           blogspot.com.

pg. 1.   C.S. Lewis, *Letters of C.S. Lewis*, W.H. Lewis, ed. (Orlando, Fla.:
           Houghton Mifflin, 1993), p. 477.

pg. 2.   *Futurama*, "Godfellas," season 3, episode 20.

pg. 3.   Augustine of Hippo, *Confessions*, bk. 10, chap. 27, in Vernon
           J. Bourke, ed., *Essential Augustine* (Indianapolis: Hackett, 1974),
           p. 148.

pg. 4.   Terry Pratchett, *Carpe Jugulum* (New York: HarperTorch, 2000),
           p. 277.

pg. 5.   Marilynne Robinson, *Gilead* (New York: Picador, 2004), p. 41.

pg. 6.   Jim Butcher, *White Nights* (New York: Penguin, 2007), p. 9.

pg. 10.   Alice Cooper, interview, *HM: The Hard Music Magazine*, 2001.

pg. 10.   Attributed to St. John Vianney.

pg. 11.   Phillip McGraw (Dr. Phil), *The Ultimate Weight Solution: The 7 Keys
           to Weight Loss Freedom* (New York: Free Press, 2004), p. 22.

pg. 11.   Thomas à Kempis, *The Imitation of Christ: A New Reading of the 1441
           Latin Autograph Manuscript*, William C. Creasey, trans. (Notre
           Dame, Ind.: Ave Maria, 2004), p. 49.

pg. 12.   Lee Strobel, *The Case for a Creator* (Grand Rapids: Zondervan,
           2004), p. 150.

pg. 13.   Alfred North Whitehead, *Modes of Thought* (New York: Free Press,
           1966), p. 168.

pg. 14.   Thomas Cathcart and Daniel Klein, *Plato and a Platypus Walk Into
           a Bar: Understanding Philosophy Through Jokes* (New York: Abrams
           Image, 2007), p. 1.

pg. 15   Roy H. Williams, Wizard of Ads podcast, www.mondaymorning-
           memo.com.

pg. 16.   John Vianney, sermon "Beware If You Have No Temptations,"
           www.philomena.org.

pg. 17.   Jeff Miller, The Curt Jester blog, http://splendoroftruth.com.

pg. 18. Jeffrey Overstreet, *Through a Screen Darkly: Looking Closer at Beauty, Truth and Evil in Movies* (Ventura, Calif.: Regal, 2007), p. 91.

pg. 18. Alexander Pope, *The Prose of Alexander Pope*, Rosemary Cowler, ed. (Hamden, Conn.: Archon, 1986), vol. 2, p. 161, as quoted in Vincent E. Barry, *The Dog Ate My Homework: Personal Responsibility, How We Avoid It and What to Do About It* (Kansas City, Mo.: Andrews and McMeel, 1997), p. 183.

pg. 19. Commander Adama, *Battlestar Galactica*, "Water," season 1, episode 2.

pg. 20. Bob Dylan, *Theme Time Radio Hour*, season 1, episode 1.

pg. 21. Will D. Campbell, *Brother to a Dragonfly* (New York: Continuum, 1977), p. 148.

pg. 21. M.F.K. Fisher, *An Alphabet for Gourmets* (New York: North Point, 1989), p. 135.

pg. 22. Dom Augustin Guillerand, *The Prayer of the Presence of God* (Wilkes-Barre, Pa.: Dimension, 1965), p. 114.

pg. 24. Gwen Bristow, *Calico Palace* (Chicago: Chicago Review, 2009), p. 179.

pg. 25. Benedict Groeschel, *There Are No Accidents: In All Things Trust in God* (Huntington, Ind.: Our Sunday Visitor, 2004), p. 89.

pg. 26. *The Princess Bride*, 20th Century Fox, 1987.

pg. 27. Michael Gruber, *Valley of the Bones* (New York: Harpertorch, 2006), p. 272.

pg. 28. G.K. Chesterton, letter to *The Times*, cited in Philip Yancey, *Soul Survivor: How Thirteen Unlikely Mentors Helped My Faith Survive the Church* (New York: Doubleday, 2001), p. 58.

pg. 28. Diane Schoemperlen, *Our Lady of the Lost and Found: A Novel of Mary, Faith and Friendship* (New York: Penguin, 2002), p. 317.

pg. 29. Attributed to Blaise Pascal.

pg. 30. Flannery O'Connor, *The Habit of Being: Letters of Flannery O'Connor* (New York: Farrar, Straus and Giroux, 1979), p. 354.

pg. 31. John C. Wright's Journal, http://johncwright.livejournal.com.

pg. 31. Jim Caviezel, Rush Limbaugh interview, February 27, 2004, www.bettnet.com.

pg. 32. Alison, "Because Parish Life Isn't Easy," Why I Am Catholic blog, February 27, 2010, http://yimcatholic.blogspot.com.

pg. 33. Gerald Weinberg, *Secrets of Consulting: A Guide to Giving and Getting Advice Successfully* (New York: Dorset House, 1986), p. 5.

pg. 33. *A Hard Day's Night*, United Artists, 1964.

pg. 34. *Pushing Daisies*, "The Fun in Funeral," season 1, episode 3.

pg. 35. *The African Queen*, Horizon Pictures, 1951.

pg. 35. *The Wizard of Oz*, Metro-Goldwyn-Mayer, 1939.

pg. 36. *The Onion* website, www.theonion.com.

pg. 37. Philip Yancey, *Reaching for the Invisible God: What Can We Expect to Find?* (Grand Rapids: Zondervan, 2000), p. 262.

pg. 38. Ronald Rolheiser, *The Holy Longing: The Search for a Christian Spirituality* (New York: Doubleday, 1999), p. 128.

pg. 39. Anthony of the Desert, Disquisition 114.

pg. 40. Judith Martin, *Miss Manners' Guide for the Turn-of-the-Millennium: Explicit, Practical and Entertaining Advice on Social, Business and Personal Etiquette* (New York: Fireside, 1990), p. 245.

pg. 40. Bonny Wolf, *Talking with My Mouth Full: Crab Cakes, Bundt Cakes and Other Kitchen Stories* (New York: St. Martin's, 2006), p. 78.

pg. 41. Dietrich Bonhoeffer, *The Cost of Discipleship* (New York: Touchstone, 1995), p. 196.

pg. 42. Padre Pio, quoted in C. Bernard Ruffin, *Padre Pio: The True Story* (Huntington, Ind.: Our Sunday Visitor, 1991), p. 143.

pg. 43. *Batman* TV series, "The Dead Ringers," season 2, episode 16.

pg. 44. L. Frank Baum, *The Road to Oz* (Chicago: Reilly & Lee, 1909), p. 184.

pg. 45. Gerard Manley Hopkins, "Pied Beauty," *Poems of Gerard Manley Hopkins* (Lawrence, Kans.: Digireads.com, 2010), p. 27.

pg. 46. Agatha Christie, *An Autobiography* (New York: Dodd Mead, 1977), p. 326.

pg. 47. *Monty Python's Life of Brian*, HandMade Films, 1979.

pg. 48. *Angel*, "Deep Down," season 4, episode 1.

pg. 49. P.D. James, *Devices and Desires* (New York: Random House, 1990), p. 325.

pg. 50. Joan Kimber, a personal friend of the author.

pg. 51. Ascribed on numerous blogs to Fr. David McAstoker, S.J., founder of Bellarmine Prep School, Tacoma, Washington.

pg. 52. *The Simpsons*, "Treehouse of Horror V," season 6, episode 6.

pg. 53.   The Summa Mamas blog, http://summamamas.stblogs.org.

pg. 53.   Fr. John Libone, St. Thomas Aquinas parish, Dallas, Texas.

pg. 53.   Elizabeth Scalia, The Anchoress blog, http://www.patheos.com/community/theanchoress.

pg. 54.   Cardinal Albino Luciani, *Illustrissimi: Letters*, William Weaver, trans. (Boston: Little, Brown, 1978), p. 50, as quoted in Francis Fernandez, *In Conversation with God: Ordinary Time: Weeks 24-34* (New York: Scepter, 2005), p. 271.

pg. 54.   Albert Einstein, *Out of My Later Years* (New York: Citadel, 1956), p. 5.

pg. 55.   Julia Child, NBC-TV, December 1, 1966.

pg. 55.   Dick Francis, *Wild Horses* (New York: Berkeley, 1994), p. 138.

pg. 56.   Leo Tolstoy, *Anna Karenina* (New York: Simon & Schuster, 2010), vol. 1, p. 5.

pg. 57.   Pope John Paul II, *Pilgrimage of Peace: Collected Speeches in Ireland and the United States* (London: Collins, 1980), p. 169.

pg. 57.   Bono, quoted at www.thunderstruck.org.

pg. 58.   Johnny Cash, *Unearthed*, American Recordings, 2003.

pg. 59.   Oscar Wilde, *The Decay of Lying* (Whitefish, Mont.: Kessinger, 2010), p. 20.

pg. 59.   Salman Rushdie, "October 2001: The Attacks on America," in *Step Across This Line: Collected Nonfiction 1992–2002* (New York: Random House, 2002), p. 338.

pg. 60.   Pope John Paul II, Angelus message, Adelaide, Australia, November 30, 1986.

pg. 61.   *A Knight's Tale*, Columbia Pictures, 2001.

pg. 63.   Dean Koontz, *Brother Odd* (New York: Bantam Dell, 2006), p. 338.

pg. 64.   Dr. Howard Thurman, http://thinkexist.com.

pg. 65.   Thomas Merton, excerpt from *Conjectures of a Guilty Bystander* in *Thomas Merton, Spiritual Master: The Essential Writings* (Mahwah, N.J.: Paulist, 1992), p. 144.

pg. 67.   Stephen King, *The Stand*, Book Club ed. (New York: Doubleday, 1978), p. 731.

pg. 68.   Madeleine L'Engle, Newbery Award acceptance speech, 1963.

pg. 68.   Rumer Godden, *China Court* (New York: Viking, 1961), p. 81.

pg. 69.   *School of Rock*, Paramount Pictures, 2003.

pg. 69.   Frank Gaebelein, "God Wants You to Enjoy the Arts," in *The Christian, the Arts, and the Truth: Regaining the Vision of Greatness* (New York: Doubleday Religious, 1997), p. 66.

pg. 70. G.K. Chesterton, "Humanitarianism and Strength," in *All Things Considered* (Fairfield, Iowa: 1st World Library, 2008), p. 153.

pg. 71. Flannery O'Connor, "Good Country People," in *A Good Man is Hard to Find and Other Stories* (Orlando, Fla.: Harcourt, 1955), p. 205.

pg. 72. *King of the Hill*, "Reborn to Be Wild," season 8, episode 2.

pg. 73. *The Incredibles*, Pixar, 2004.

pg. 74. Michael Crichton, *Jurassic Park* (New York: Ballantine, 1990), p. 305.

pg. 75. *Star Wars*, 20th Century Fox, 1977.

pg. 77. Peter Laws, The Flicks That Church Forgot podcast, *Evilspeak*, episode 14, www.theflicksthatchurchforgot.com.

pg. 78. Madeleine L'Engle, *A Wrinkle in Time* (New York: Square Fish, 2009), p. 229.

pg. 78. Pray-As-You-Go podcast, http://www.pray-as-you-go.org.

pg. 80. *A Fish Called Wanda*, Metro-Goldwyn-Mayer, 1988.

pg. 81. Bill Maher, *Newsweek* interview, quoted in Tony Rossi, "Christian Love Casts Out Cockeyed Priorities," *National Catholic Register*, May 4, 2010, www.ncregister.com.

pg. 81. John Chrysostom, Homily 10 on 1 Timothy, Migne, PG. 62.551, as quoted in Pope John XXIII, *Princeps Pastorum*, Encyclical on the Missions, Native Clergy, and Lay Participation, promulgated November 28, 1959, www.newadvent.org.

pg. 82. Benedict Groeschel, *Heaven in Our Hands: Receiving the Blessings We Long For* (Ann Arbor, Mich.: Charis, 1994), p. 107.

pg. 83. John Vianney, quoted in John Edward Bonen, ed., *The Spirit of the Cure of Ars*, Alfred Monnin, trans. (Charleston, S.C.: BiblioBazaar, 2008), p. 201.

pg. 83. Robert R. Chase, *The Game of Fox and Lion* (New York: Del Rey, 1986), p. 243.

pg. 84. *Harvey*, Universal International Pictures, 1950.

pg. 85. *Millions*, Fox Searchlight Pictures, 2004.

pg. 86. Liz Parker, in *A Confidential Agent*, "A Husband Scorned," BBC Audio Drama, 2007.

pg. 87. *Joan of Arcadia*, pilot episode, 2003.

pg. 88. Josemaría Escrivá, *The Way: The Essential Classic by Opus Dei's Founder* (New York: Image, 2006), p. 1.

pg. 88. Lao-tzu, *Tao Te Ching: The New Translation from Tao Te Ching: The Definitive Edition*, Jonathan Star, trans. (London: Jeremy P. Tarcher/Penguin, 2001), p. 83.

pg. 89. Michael Baruzzini, "The Universal, the Particular, and How Roman Catholics Think," CatholicExchange.com, May 11, 2010.

pg. 90. Attributed to Mark Twain.

pg. 91. Caryll Houselander, *Caryll Houselander: Essential Writings* (Maryknoll, N.Y.: Orbis, 2005), p. 106.

pg. 91. Attributed to Roseanne Barr at shedyourweight.com and elsewhere.

pg. 92. T.M. Camp, *Assam & Darjeeling* (Grand Rapids: Aurohn, 2010), p. 184.

pg. 93. Johann Wolfgang Von Goethe, quoted in Betsy Flot, *Inspiration Station* (Bloomington, Ind.: Xlibris, 2010), p. 398.

pg. 93. Terry Pratchett, *Lords and Ladies* (New York: HarperTorch, 1992), p. 1.

pg. 93. Dave Thomas, www.brainyquote.com.

pg. 93. Woody Allen, http://booksandbars.com.

pg. 94. Quentin Crisp, www.goodreads.com.

pg. 96. *Firefly*, pilot episode, 2002.

pg. 97. *About a Boy*, Universal Pictures, 2002.

pg. 97. Dorothy Day, *The Long Loneliness: The Autobiography of the Legendary Social Activist* (New York: Harper & Row, 1952), p. 290.

pg. 99. Author's review of Robert Sawyer, *Calculating God*, and Sawyer's response, SFFaudio.com, June 5, 2008.

pg. 100. Ayn Rand, *The Fountainhead* (New York: Plume, 1999), p. 368.

pg. 100. H.G. Wells, *The War of the Worlds* (Madison, Wis.: Cricket House, 2010), p. 77.

pg. 101. Barbara Hambly, *The Unschooled Wizard: Sun Wolf—Book One: The Ladies of Mandrigyn; Book Two: The Witches of Wenshar*, Book Club ed. (Garden City, N.Y.: Nelson Doubleday, 1987), p. 253.

pg. 102. John Newton, "Amazing Grace," 1779.

pg. 103. Kathryn Stockett, *The Help* (New York: G.P. Putnam, 2009), p. 49.

pg. 104. Lewis Carroll, *Through the Looking Glass (And What Alice Found There)* (Boston: Thomas Y. Crowell, 1893), p. 150.

pg. 105. *House, M.D.*, "Three Stories," episode 121.

pg. 106. Samuel Butler, *The Note-Books of Samuel Butler* (Charleston, S.C.: BiblioBazaar, 2006), p. 220.

pg. 106.   Gene Hill, "Hill Country" column, *Field & Stream* magazine.

pg. 106.   Faculty of the University of Navarre, *The Navarre Bible: The Pentateuch* (Dublin: Four Courts, 2000), p. 328.

pg. 106.   Terry Hershey, *The Power of Pause* (Chicago: Loyola, 2009), p. 99.

pg. 108.   M. Eugene Boylan, *This Tremendous Lover*, rev. ed. (Notre Dame, Ind.: Christian Classics, 2009), p. 250.

pg. 110.   John Cantius, also known as John of Kanty, quoted at Catholic Online, www.catholic.org.

pg. 110.   Alfred Bester, *The Stars My Destination* (New York: Random House, 1996), p. 256.

pg. 111.   Steve Martin, quoted at http://thinkexist.com.

pg. 111.   Paul Klee, quoted at www.brainyquote.com.

pg. 112.   Jeremy Hsu, "The Secrets of Storytelling: Why We Love a Good Yarn," *Scientific American Mind*, August 2008.

pg. 112.   Mother Teresa, *No Greater Love* (Novato, Calif.: New World Library, 1989), p. 55.

pg. 113.   *Cool Runnings*, Walt Disney Pictures, 1989.

pg. 114.   Mark Schweizer, runner-up, detective category, Bulwer-Lytton Fiction Contest 2007, quoted at www.bulwer-lytton.com.

pg. 115.   John Foster Hall, "The Parson Addresses His Flock," 1923 recording.

pg. 116.   "Daily Quote from St. Katharine Drexel," August 24, 2010, www.integratedcatholiclife.org.

pg. 116.   Pope Benedict XVI (Joseph Cardinal Ratzinger) and Pete Seewald, *God and the World: A Conversation with Pete Seewald* (San Francisco: Ignatius, 2002), p. 187.

pg. 117.   *The Simpsons*, "Trash of the Titans," season 9, episode 22.

pg. 117.   Miss Manners, *The Washington Post*, June 23, 2010.

pg. 118.   Frances Hodgson Burnett, *A Little Princess* (New York: HarperCollins, 1987), p. 140.

pg. 119.   Henryk Sienkiewicz, *Quo Vadis*, W.S. Juniczak, trans. (New York: Hippocrene, 2004), p. 158.

pg. 120.   Lars Walker, www.brandywinebooks.net, October 31, 2009.

pg. 120.   *This Is Spinal Tap*, Embassy Pictures, 1984.

pg. 121.   David Morrison, *Sed Contra* blog (now defunct).

pg. 122.   C.S. Lewis, *The Four Loves* (Orlando, Fla.: Harcourt Brace, 1988), p. 121.

pg. 123.   Judy Squier, www.squierfamily.net, quoting Richard Bach, *Illusions: The Adventure of a Reluctant Messiah* (New York: Dell, 1998), p. 134.

pg. 123.   Juda Myers, quoted at Coming Home blog, http://gerardnadal. com. Also see Juda Myers Freedom Ministry, http://www. juda4praise.com.

pg. 123.   David Manuel, quoted at Jennifer's Favorite Links, http://jen-niferslinks.blogspot.com.

pg. 124.   Susanna Clarke, *Jonathan Strange & Mr. Norrell* (New York: Tor, 2006), p. 389.

pg. 125.   Alasdair Stuart, Pseudopod, the sound of horror podcast, http://pseudopod.org.

pg. 126.   See Hilton Kramer, ed., *The New Criterion Reader: The First Five Years* (New York: Free Press, 1988), p. 124.

pg. 127.   Bernhard Riemann, quoted in Kathleen Norris, *The Cloister Walk* (New York: Riverhead, 1997), p. 217.

pg. 128.   Eric Brown, *"Fides Quarens Intellectum,"* The American Catholic blog, http://the-american-catholic.com.

pg. 128.   *30 Rock*, "The Fighting Irish," season 1, episode 17.

pg. 128.   Winston Churchill, Speech, House of Commons, February 27, 1945.

pg. 129.   Lois, on *Malcolm in the Middle*, "Shame," season 1, episode 4.

pg. 130.   Edward Abbey, *A Voice Crying in the Wilderness (Vox Clamantis in Deserto): Notes from a Secret Journal* (New York: St. Martin's, 1985), p. 17.

pg. 131.   Patricia Volk, *Stuffed: Adventures of a Restaurant Family* (New York: Knopf Doubleday, 2002), p. 98.

pg. 132.   Charles Swindoll, *The Mystery of God's Will* (Nashville: Thomas Nelson, 1999), p. 184.

pg. 133.   Henri Nouwen, *Here and Now: Living in the Spirit* (New York: Crossroad, 1994), p. 143.

pg. 134.   John da Fiesole, Disputations blog, http://disputations. blogspot.com.

pg. 135.   Judith Viorst, quoted at www.goodreads.com.

pg. 135.   Roald Dahl, *The Twits* (London: Penguin, 2004), p. 8.

pg. 136. J.R.R. Tolkien, letter, as quoted in Steven D. Greydanus, "Faith and Fantasy: Tolkien the Catholic, *The Lord of the Rings*, and Peter Jackson's Film Trilogy," www.decentfilms.com.

pg. 137. Lars Gren, quoted in Elisabeth Elliot, *Love Has a Price Tag* (Chappaqua, N.Y.: Christian Herald Books, 1981), p. 97.

pg. 138. Hermann Cohen, quoted by Raniero Cantalamessa in a homily, "A Woman Came With an Alabaster Flask of Ointment," on June 17, 2007, www.cantalamessa.org.

pg. 139. Dorothy Day, quoted in Evelyn Birge Vitz, *A Continual Feast: A Cookbook to Celebrate the Joys of Family and Faith* (New York: Harper & Row, 1985), p. 61.

pg. 140. Mark Shea, Catholic and Enjoying It blog, http://markshea.blogspot.com.

pg. 141. *In Bruges*, Focus Features, 2008.

pg. 143. Larry Niven and Jerry Pournelle, *Inferno* (New York: Orb, 2008), p. 173.

pg. 144. Robert Farrar Capon, *The Supper of the Lamb* (New York: Doubleday, 1969), p. 7.

pg. 146. Mother Marie des Douleurs, quoted in *Magnificat* magazine, www.magnificat.net.

pg. 146. Charles Chaput, address, "The King's Good Servant: Living the Faith in the Church and the World," September 30, 2004, www.archden.org.

pg. 148. Raniero Cantalamessa, *Loving the Church: Scriptural Meditations for the Papal Household*, Gilberto Cavazos-González and Amanda Quantz, trans. (Cincinnati: Servant, 2003), p. 45.

Index

ABOUT THE AUTHOR

JULIE DAVIS is the creator of the Happy Catholic blog, podcasts novels at Forgotten Classics and foodblogs at Meanwhile, Back in the Kitchen. She and her husband live in Dallas and have two grown daughters.